LIFE IN CHRIST

By the same author:

God Alive: Priorities in Pastoral Theology (DLT)
The Gospel is for Everyone (Church Union)
Firmly I Believe and Truly (Mowbray)

Also contributor to:

A Critique of Eucharistic Agreement (SPCK)
The Cross and the Bomb (Mowbray)
Is Christianity Credible? (Epworth Press)
The Price of Peace
Unholy Warfare: Church and the Bomb (Blackwell)

LIFE IN CHRIST

by

Graham Leonard

Bishop of London

MOWBRAY
LONDON & OXFORD

Copyright © Graham Leonard 1986

First published 1986
by A.R. Mowbray & Co. Ltd,
Saint Thomas House, Becket Street,
Oxford, OX1 1SJ

All rights reserved. No part of this publication
may be reproduced, stored in a retrieval system,
or transmitted, in any form or by any means,
electronic, menchanical, photocopying, recording,
or otherwise, without the prior permission in writing
from the publisher, A. R. Mowbray & Co. Ltd.

Typeset by Comersgate Art Studios Ltd, 52 St Clements
Street, Oxford, OX1 4AG
Printed in Great Britain by Cox and Wyman Ltd., Reading

British Library Cataloguing in Publication Data

Leonard, Graham
Life in Christ.—(Mowbrays popular
Christian paperbacks)
1. Christian life
I. Title
248.4 BV4501.2

ISBN 0-264-67087-6

To
Gordon and Peggy
with love

ACKNOWLEDGEMENTS

Scriptural quotations are from the New English Bible unless otherwise stated.

Prayers after the Chapters (except for Psalm 8 after Chapter 1) are from *My God, My Glory*, E. Milner-White, SPCK.

Extracts from *Collected Poems 1909-62* by T.S. Eliot are reprinted by permission of Faber and Faber Ltd.

Preface

The Life of a Christian

A human being yes
But now in Christ
Not just redeemed by Him
To live for Him as best I may
But by His Love and Power
To share His Life
In body, mind and soul
That I may live in Him and He in me:
So that I may His praise express,
His joys acquire
Suffer with Him
And pray with Him
That, in Him, by His Love I may be moved
And of His Love my life may speak.

To live in Christ by his grace, as I have tried to express it in the verse above, is to live in a relationship to him which extends to every aspect of our lives. Its meaning and significance are not to be found simply in what we think, what we do or what we say, as if such things constituted our Christian life. It is a relationship of love in which every thought and act and word should be an expression of love in an ever-deepening and joyful obedience as we discern the will of God.

In my last book, *Firmly I Believe and Truly*, I sought to expound the meaning of what God did in Christ to make it possible for us to share his life and which should determine the character of our life in Christ. It is about that character that I write in the present book, in the hope and prayer that it will help to deepen our relationship with our living Lord.

+ GRAHAM LONDIN:

Contents

Preface — *page* vii

1. Human Life and Christian Life — 1
2. The Life of Christ — 11
3. The Life of Christ Shared — 18
4. The Body of Christ — 28
5. The Mind of a Christian — 39
6. The Body of a Christian — 53
7. The Heart of a Christian — 72
8. In the Image of God — 84

Notes — 95

For Further Reading — 97

1
Human Life and Christian Life

If you say that you are going to talk about living as a Christian today, most people, including many Christians, will assume that you are going to speak about the particular things which Christians do, or the attitudes which they adopt. Some will suppose that you are going to speak about such activities as going to church, praying or taking an active part in the life of your local church. The minds of others will turn immediately to what you do for other people as the way of carrying out the command to love your neighbour. Others will think of the line which you take on the moral and social problems of our time, and whether you are actively engaged in trying to press it on others.

Christians are, certainly, committed to worship and above all to take part in the Service which Christ has commanded us to continue, the Eucharist or Holy Communion, which should be the centre of their lives. They will also pray, as the expression of the relationship which God has given them to himself in Christ. Some will also be called to particular work in their local church. Likewise, Christians have a duty to love their neighbour, a duty which will involve doing things for other people. Christians should also be prepared to think about the meaning of their Christian belief and the effect it should have on their attitude to social and moral problems and, when occasions arise or demand, to commend it and be prepared to stand up for it.

But these activities do not constitute our Christian life, nor do they make it, any more than doing the things which human beings do make our human life. Human life is a gift, ultimately from God, which we receive at birth. We eat, drink, sleep, speak, think, work and rest, because they are necessary for the development of that human life. Such activities are proper and necessary if we are to grow as human beings and if we are going to be able to live our human life at the deepest level by learning to love, to create, to make decisions, to exercise compassion, to take responsibility and to experience joy.

If we are to be able to grow in that way, we have to remember and take account of what we are as human beings, and, above all, that we are persons in whom body, mind and spirit are united together in a single being. This fact makes great demands upon us. As a result, throughout history, people have tried to find ways of living as human beings, by concentrating on one or other aspect of our human nature, as if it were the only one that really mattered. So, some have concentrated on the material or bodily side of our being and on its satisfaction. This attitude is expressed in the saying, 'Eat, drink and be merry for tomorrow we die', and it is an attitude which is very common at the present time in the West. Others have concentrated on the spiritual element in our nature, and have often done so in a way which implies or even states that the bodily element in us is essentially evil, to be kept rigidly under control in this life, and from it we shall mercifully be delivered at death. Others have put all the emphasis on man's ability to use his reason and to engage in creative activity. Such an emphasis leads very easily to elitism, by which the human race becomes divided into those who are capable of intellectual and creative activity and those who are not; the latter becoming, in effect, the slaves of the former. It also leads to that attitude by which man believes that he is lord of creation and can exploit it as he will, without taking account of its pattern and structure. Others lay stress on the moral nature of man but by seeking to compel people to act morally deny them freedom and the ultimate responsibility of man to make moral judgements.

Just as in any living organism, the various organs and cells must act in co-operation, each functioning in its own proper way, if the organism is to be healthy, so in man, the body, mind and spirit have to be exercised in co-operation, if he is to live a truly human life.

The Christian life is also a gift of God. It is not something which we achieve by our own efforts. The Bible, especially the New Testament, makes that very clear. How it is given will be considered later. For the moment, I want to emphasize that it is a gift of God. Our Lord himself speaks of the need for people to be born again and St Paul likens becoming a Christian to being made a new creature. He contrasts the life which we possess as those born 'in Adam', as human beings, with the new life which is given to us when we are reborn 'in Christ', that is, as Christian beings. Just as, born in Adam, we are members of the human race, so, 'in Christ', we are members of his body which includes the new race of all who are united to him. I shall consider later what membership of the body of Christ means. For the moment, I want to concentrate on one point. The Christian life, that is life in Christ, is not given to us as a kind of second life which we have to live out side by side with our ordinary human life. It is given to us in order that we may live in the way God intended human beings to live. To live in Christ is to live in union not only with the one who redeemed the world but with the one by whom it was made, and who knows how we should live as human beings.

'In the beginning was the Word . . . by whom all things were made which were made . . . and the Word was made flesh and dwelt among us' (John 1 AV). To live in Christ means living in a way which also expresses and reflects what we are as human beings. In other words, it means living in Christ as that unity of body, mind and spirit, which is characteristic of man. So St Paul can describe man in Christ as in the process of becoming holy and blameless 'spirit, soul and body' (1 Thess. 5.23).

For this reason, before considering how as Christians we live in mind, body and spirit, I shall first look at what the Scriptures say about man, his nature and his destiny. They give us a vision of man in his relationships with God, with his fellow-men and with the whole created world. In the first place, man is created by God, to whom he owes his existence and upon whom he depends. Man exists because he has or is a body which is part of the created world. Unlike the Greeks who looked upon a human being as a spirit imprisoned in a body, the Hebrews regarded the human person as an animated body. The 'soul' was not contrasted with the 'body'. It was the 'soul' which was to control the activities of the whole person. A man was a man because he shared in the flesh substance common to all men and to animals. It was this which gave him his existence and bound him in his relationships to his neighbour and to nature. It was in and through that body that man was called upon to live as a soul who is capable of entering into a relationship to God who has created him. In other words, what we might call man's spiritual life is to be lived by him as a whole human being of body, mind and spirit.

Scripture tells us that man is made in 'the image of God', which means that, in a special way, he is intended to reflect the nature of God. In one sense, man is made in the image of God because he is part of the created world, which is an expression of the wisdom and glory of God. But man has unique qualities and is called upon to enter into a relationship with God who has made him, which is not possible for inanimate objects or for animals.

What are the qualities which make it possible for man to enter into that relationship? The most important is the ability to choose. It is the most important because it is essential if we are able to love. No one can be compelled to love, for love depends upon a response which is not forced and is freely given. Loving, however, involves other choices which man is free to make. He can choose between right and wrong, between good and evil, between beauty and ugliness, between justice and injustice. To love someone truly, man has to choose the right, the good, the beautiful and the just for those whom he seeks to love. What is especially significant for man is that he can and does choose to do so even when it makes great demands upon him and involves putting those whom he loves first, at what seems to be disadvantage or cost to himself.

Some people deny that man possesses this power of choice and maintain that he is wholly determined in what he does by forces beyond his control, such as his genetical make-up, his environment or his upbringing. In practice, that is not how man behaves. Indeed, those who hold such a view deny it themselves by choosing to press it on others, assuming that other people are capable of choosing to adopt a particular way no matter what their background or upbringing. Determinists have no reason or right to do so if their views, and those of others, are determined by factors outside their control. There is no doubt, of course, that as human beings we are affected by such things as our background, the nature and state of our bodies and the society in which we live, which limits the choices open to us. Likewise we are affected and limited by the decisions we have taken in the past and the decisions taken by others. But the fact that our choices are limited does not mean that we do not have any. If I go out to buy a pair of shoes and have only £20 to spend, it does not mean that I am not free to choose to buy some or to choose which to buy. It means that I cannot choose to buy a pair which costs more than £20. In one sense, all our choices are limited in this kind of way. Human freedom is not unlimited.

One reason why this should be so is because we live as part of the physical world which provides the framework in which we can choose. We can rely upon it as predictable, and this gives us freedom. We find it impossible to contemplate a world in which things would be ever-changing to suit the desires of everyone. We just cannot imagine a situation in which every hill would be downhill for us when walking in one direction and also downhill for someone else walking in the opposite direction, or of a car made of material which would be hard as long as it was being used for our benefit but soft as soon as someone was using it to run us down. Another reason why our freedom is restricted is because we are members of the community of mankind. What we choose to do and the way we act affects everyone else. I find it very disturbing to think about the effects which my anger, bitterness or lack of charity may have had far beyond the immediate community in which I live. The way I have treated or reacted to one person may well affect the way he or she treats others, and so on. Human relationships are not just one to one or confined to a family. They are part of an infinite web of interacting relationships. This fact presents us with the problem of what is called 'the one and the many'. Conscious of ourselves as individual and unique persons and properly concerned to develop our personal identity, we have to live in community, establish personal relationships with others and accept our dependence upon them by the exercise of our wills.

To anticipate, I would at this stage just say that the Christian practices of penitence, forgiveness and prayer play a very important part in enabling us to live in this very human situation.

So man exhibits pairs of qualities with which he has to live as a human being. He is both body and spirit. He is at once dependent and restricted, yet possesses his own individuality and freedom. He is a human being at every stage of life and yet is in the process of becoming – of living out what it really means to be human. These qualities make great demands upon us, yet we must never forget that they also provide the potential for the glorious possibilities which are open to human beings, alone among the created world. 'What is man, that thou art mindful of him: and the son of man, that thou visitest him? Thou madest him lower than the angels: to crown him with glory and worship'. (Ps. 8 4–5 BCP)

But man is faced not only with the demands of living to his potential. From what I have written about the nature of the world in which he lives, it follows that it is an ambiguous world. It is ordered, infinitely varied, creative and beautiful. Yet it is also wounded, tragic, and demonic. Water is life-giving. It refreshes and can be beautiful. Yet it can also drown and can appear threatening and destructive. Fire can warm us and give us delicious food. Yet it can also destroy and kill. The ambiguity of the world becomes tragic and demonic when man ignores its pattern and structure, fails to respect it and exploits it for his own ends, without realizing or accepting what results his actions will have on the world itself or on others.

But the trouble does not lie simply in the impersonal world which can at once be destructive and life-giving. For man, it lies in that fatal flaw which disposes him to choose the evil rather than the good. It is a flaw which not only disposes him to choose evil, but also affects and corrupts his natural and good instincts. As a result man ceases to act in a way which reflects his nature as a unity of body, mind and spirit. When he is called to exercise compassion, his heart runs away with his head and instead of compassion, he offers condonation. Likewise his mind can seek to exercise undue domination, so that he applies what he judges to be right without respect for the liberty of others. His zeal becomes corrupted into fanaticism and a desire to manipulate others. So also, the body can press its claims against those of the mind and the spirit. We allow the desire for physical pleasure to take over. The desire to rest and recreate becomes idleness and sloth. Faithfulness to a partner and to children is swept aside by the pressure of infatuation.

We all experience the pressure for these things to happen. It is the pressure which led St Paul to write, 'The good that I would I do not, the evil that I would not, that I do.' The pressure is not limited to influencing us in respect of one sin or group of sins such as is sometimes supposed, with those connected with sex. It affects the whole of our being and everything we do, including our religion. We are constantly tempted to think of God not as to be worshipped and loved but in terms of his usefulness to us. It is this pressure which theologians have described as 'original sin'. This is a misleading name, for we naturally think of sin as deliberately doing something which is wrong. For this reason the term 'original sin' is often regarded as meaning that we have committed sinful acts and therefore, not surprisingly, people regard it as absurd when applied to very small babies. It is a technical phrase describing the universal human experience of which St Paul speaks and to which the Articles of the Church of England refer when they say that man is 'of his own nature inclined to evil'. The origin of this bias within us is a mystery about which we shall never be able to be dogmatic. It is impossible for us to get outside it and even our thinking about it is affected by it. For my part, I find that the most profitable way of thinking about it is to reflect on the fact that, in the created world as a whole, it is always easy to destroy or pull down whereas much effort is needed to create or build. One of the characteristics of good is that by its very nature it is constructive, whereas evil is by its very nature destructive and leads to disintegration. God has created the universe and man, not in a static state but with a process of becoming. So St Paul can speak of the way in which creation is to be freed from the shackles of mortality and enter upon the liberty and splendour of the sons of God. So 'it groans in all its parts as if in the pangs of childbirth'. (Romans 8.21,22) However, what matters for the purpose of living in Christ is not speculation about its origins but the recognition of its existence. It is as we take seriously the pressures upon us, that we can become more and more aware of the gifts of grace in Christ which enable us to overcome them.

As far as man is concerned, the pressure is directed towards making us live and act as if we believed that to be truly human we must reject our dependence upon God, upon each other and upon the created world, and behave as if each of us were judge in our own cause. Self-centredness is at the heart of sin and to live in Christ means learning to die to that self-centredness, to rise to a new life, which is centred upon God and overflows into love for our neighbour and respect for the world in which we live.

Human life presents problems of living in time, though able to transcend it, of living as an individual yet essentially as a member of the community, of exercising our freedom but within the limitations provided by our bodies and the physical world. The Christian who lives in Christ is not freed from these problems but is given the grace to live with them so that human life itself is lived to the full in a way which is true to its essential nature, and lived for its true end which is that of fellowship with the living God.

A PSALM OF PRAISE

O Lord our Governor, how excellent is thy Name in all the world : thou that has set thy glory above the heavens!

2 Out of the mouth of very babes and sucklings hast thou ordained strength, because of thine enemies : that thou mightest still the enemy, and the avenger.

3 For I will consider thy heavens, even the works of thy fingers : the moon and the stars, which thou hast ordained.

4 What is man, that thou art mindful of him : and the son of man, that thou visitest him?

5 Thou madest him lower than the angels : to crown him with glory and worship.

6 Thou makest him to have dominion of the works of thy hands : and thou hast put all things in subjection under his feet.

7 All sheep and oxen : yea, and the beasts of the field;

8 The fowls of the air, and the fishes of the sea : and whatsoever walketh through the paths of the seas.

9 O Lord our Governor : how excellent is thy Name in all the world!

Psalm 8

2

The Life of Christ

'Jesus was born at Bethlehem in Judaea during the reign of Herod' (Matt. 2.1). By that act the second person of the Blessed Trinity, God the Son, came to share our human life in all its aspects. He took from Mary his mother 'all that appertains to the perfection of our human nature'. St John put the meaning of the event very directly when he said that the Word who was God 'was made flesh'. Why did he do so? That is the crucial question. In my book *Firmly I Believe and Truly* I wrote about what we believe when we say that God became man and how we can think about him being both at the same time. To appreciate what it means to live in Christ, we must try to understand the purpose for which he came.

In the first place we must recognize that, as I have said, he came to share our human life in all its aspects. He did not simply appear on earth in human form so that he could, as it were, cure us from outside. He came to live as a human being and as such, to live in the way God intended man to live. That meant sharing all those characteristics of human life which I considered in the last chapter.

First, as man he was body, mind and spirit. He experienced human life, as we all do, through and in his body, with the limitations which we experience. He could not be everywhere at the same time. He had to carry out his mission in a particular place at a particular time. His ministry was limited to those whom he visited, called and met when they came to him. For this reason, he chose the twelve, whom he specially trained and commissioned so that they could carry on his work after his death. The effects of what he was going to do would not miraculously and suddenly be, as it were, applied to everyone whether they liked it or not. He came for the benefit of human beings, in particular places and particular times.

We know from the accounts of his life in the Gospels that he experienced the demands of the body which human beings experience. He was hungry and needed food. He became tired. His emotions found expression in his body. He wept in sorrow and groaned in anguish. In the garden of Gethsemane, where he experienced the greatest temptation, his agony found physical expression as he sweated blood.

In his body he experienced the beauty of the created world. He used his appreciation of the flowers of the field to speak about God the Father. He appreciated sunrise and sunset and the beauty of a fine pearl. He knew the joys of special friendships. He shared in the feasts by which people have always marked special occasions, so much so that he was accused of being a 'gluttonous man and a wine-bibber'. As man, he also experienced the tragedies of life, the bereaved mother, the parents with a handicapped child, the disaster when the tower of Siloam fell down killing eighteen innocent people, the woman with a chronic disease. He experienced personal sorrow: the sorrow of being misunderstood, the sorrow of experiencing disloyalty, the sorrow of being deserted, the sorrow of being rejected.

He also experienced temptation in a way which we shall never understand. The accounts of his temptations in the wilderness reveal their subtle nature. Appeal is made to his physical needs, but he is also tempted to achieve his purpose in ways which are not those of God and which, if he gave in to them, would mean that he was setting himself up against the Father. The Gospel accounts reveal that his temptations were not limited to the period in the wilderness and to Gethsemane but assailed him throughout his earthly life, not least when questioned by his enemies. In the Epistle to the Hebrews, his identification with us is movingly described. 'The children of a family share the same flesh and blood; and so he too shared ours, so that through death he might break the power of him who had death as his command, that is, the devil; and might liberate those who, through fear of death, had all their lifetime been in servitude. . . . And therefore he had to be made like these brothers of his in every way, so that he might be merciful and faithful as their high priest before God, to expiate the sins of the people. For since he himself has passed through the test of suffering, he is able to help those who are meeting their test now' (Heb. 2.14–18). 'For ours is not a high priest unable to sympathize with our weaknesses, but one who, because of his likeness to us, has been tested in every way, only without sin'. (Heb. 4.15)

As a man, body, mind and spirit, Jesus lived our human life in perfect obedience to God. He, himself, said that his meat and drink was to do God's will. He said that he 'Came not to do his own will, but the will of him who sent him' (St John 6.38). From 'his coming into the world' (Hebrews 10.5) until on the cross 'he bowed his head and gave up his spirit' (St John 19.30), he willed what God willed in every kind of human situation. When St Paul tells us that we must have the mind of Christ, it is upon the obedience of Christ that he lays particular emphasis. 'Have this mind among yourselves, which is yours in Christ Jesus, who, though he was in the form of God, did not count equality with God a thing to be grasped, but emptied himself, taking the form of a servant, being born in the likeness of men. And being found in human form he humbled himself and became obedient unto death, even death on a cross'. (Phil. 2.5–8 RSV)

He was recognized as having authority in a unique way. 'The people were astounded at his teaching, for, unlike the doctors of the law, he taught with a note of authority' (Mark 1.22). 'No man ever spoke as this man speaks' (John 7.46). But the Gospels also make it clear that he was recognized as a man who himself was under authority and whose overriding concern was to obey the will of God. The only point at which Christ contrasts his will with that of God is in the garden of Gethsemane when he is tempted to go his own way and reject that of God. As we shall see, Christ fulfilled the divine law by obeying it from the heart, and in matters such as divorce, murder, adultery, he accepted that law while making clear its inner demands, in such a way that on one recorded occasion, the disciples were so astonished that they asked, if that be so, who could be saved.

Jesus, as man, though not created, being God, shared our creatureliness, that is, our dependence upon God and the fact that we are created to obey God's will. For the first time, someone lived as man, whose will was identified with that of God at every point, whatever the cost to himself. 'He learned obedience in the school of suffering' (Hebrews 5.8). His acceptance of the divine will was in sharp contrast to the prevalent attitude of today, certainly in the West. As I have written elsewhere, 'one characteristic of our society . . . which underlies all its characteristics like a ground bass is the attitude that suffering is the worst evil and that anything, however morally wrong, is justified if it appears to relieve suffering'.[1] I said that it might 'seem surprising and illogical that the infliction of suffering on others to get one's own way should be on the increase at a time when suffering is regarded as the greatest evil. It should be neither, for the desire to avoid suffering at all costs springs from a self-centredness and a failure to love. In a fallen world, in which suffering will not just go away, it means demanding that everyone else should bear the cost of suffering. The desire to avoid it leads to an insensitiveness towards the suffering of others.'2 Jesus in his total commitment to obedience, by contrast, bore the cost of it in himself, while at the same time sharing the deepest compassion towards those who were suffering and acting to relieve them.

Jesus Christ was the first and only one since the human race began never to choose to obey himself rather than God. Human beings are made to be social beings, living in community, and enabled to do so by a common obedience to God. In fact, we are all of us anti-social, each of us wanting to live for what we judge to be our own best interests. Jesus lived in the one way which could keep society from falling apart through selfishness and self-centredness. But he did much more.

Though 'taking the form of a servant', Jesus did not obey simply as a matter of duty, even of the most noble and costly kind. As God the Son, the second person of the Blessed Trinity, he lives in eternity in a perfect relationship of love to God the Father, wholly giving himself to the Father in love and receiving from the Father in love. That relationship is still perfectly expressed in the incarnate life of the Son. Because loving God first requires obedience to his will, such obedience is the basis of the love of Jesus to the Father in his earthly life. But it is offered in love and is the expression of that love.

So in the Gospels we find two ways of speaking about what Jesus came to do, two ways which are interwoven with each other. Jesus speaks about the kingdom of God which is inaugurated on earth by his presence and evident in his life and acts. In them the rule of God as creator and Lord is perfectly accepted, and his love and power are to be seen and heard by those who have eyes to see and ears to hear. At the same time Jesus speaks of the unique relationship which he has with God the Father. The baptism of Jesus and his transfiguration witness to it. It is also evident in his teaching, his prayers and the way in which he spoke about and addressed God. 'Everything is entrusted to me by my Father; and no one knows the Son but the Father, and no one knows the Father but the Son and those to whom the Son may choose to reveal him' (Matthew 11.27). The farewell discourses, particularly that in John 17, express with the utmost sensitivity the relationship between the Father, the Son and the Spirit as the passion proceeds from their mutual love.

Dr John Lowe, in his commentary on the Lord's Prayer, says that among the Jews at the time of our Lord, their understanding of God as Father 'was qualified to the extent that this was only one way among others of regarding God. In their literature, while "Father" does appear, "Lord" and "King" remain much the more common expressions. With Jesus the fact that God is Father is the central and all-determining truth.'[3] He says that 'the new situation created by the coming of Christ is a new revelation of the nature of God's Fatherhood . . . God's decisive intervention at the end of the days shows in act what his being the Father means. Above all the full and final revelation of God's fatherhood has come through the Son, *the* Son *par excellence*. Peter's recognition and confession of the Son of the living God is the gift of "my Father in heaven" (Matthew 16.17). The absolute fatherhood of God is not, so to speak, an insight of natural theology, but is demonstrated through the Son.'[4]

God who is absolute sovereign is shown in Christ to be also absolute Father. His will is done wholly and perfectly in Christ, who offers it to the Father as the free and willing response of love in complete trust.

THE DIVINE MAJESTY

SHEW me thy majesty, O Lord God
    the majesty of thy glory,
but once, but for an instant,
    and it suffices.

YET shewn it, thou hast:
    not once, nor twice,
        not for a moment, nor an hour, nor a day,
            but hourly, daily, always;
shewn not one, but many majesties
        unsearchable, inexpressible,
            majesty upon majesty and the fulness of glory,
IN JESUS CHRIST THY SON OUR LORD.

IN JESUS CHRIST, THY SON, OUR LORD:
    whom having seen, we have seen the Father:
    whom seeing, we see GOD:
    whom we may not only see,
        but know, and accompany, and love:
who chooses and comes to dwell among us,
    to make his abode in us,
        full of grace and truth.

3

The Life of Christ Shared

Why did God become man? An early Christian saint, Irenaeus, who was Bishop of Lyons and lived from about AD 130–200, answered this question quite simply: 'Because of his boundless love, he became what we are in order that he might make us what he is.' And St Athanasius, who fought, almost single handed at one point, during the fourth century for the truth about the person of Christ, put it as follows in his book on the incarnation: 'The Word of God came in His own Person, because it was He alone, the Image of the Father, Who could recreate man made after the Image.'[1]

Simple and direct though these answers seem, they can be, and are, misunderstood particularly at the present time. They can be taken simply to mean that Jesus lived and died to be our example so that we can try to imitate the way he lived and become like God. Of course, we have to learn to become like him but to see him just as our example is woefully inadequate judged by the teaching of the New Testament. Those who take such a view also often minimize the importance of the atoning death of Christ for the forgiveness of sins. It is, however, possible to lay great stress upon the significance and necessity of the cross and still regard it as doing no more than liberating us to try to live our human life in such a way that we eventually come to know and live with God in the world to come.

It is clear from the whole of the New Testament that the purpose for which Christ lived, died and rose again was not to reveal a new morality or provide a new way of helping man to discover God by his own efforts. Our Lord was incarnate to be nothing less than the first of a new race, a race of men and women, forgiven by God, reconciled to him, and unbreakably joined with God by their union with Christ. He became one of us that we might become part of him. In him men and women can be new creatures. In Christ God offers to man something which he did not have before and which he cannot achieve by his own efforts. It is in this sense that we can and should speak of eternal life as being the gift of God, offered to man not because of what he has done to merit it but because, in his boundless love, God wants men and women to share his life. That is the Gospel of the New Testament. God gives to man a new relationship to himself, a relationship which is to be lived out in this life but which will abide for ever. It is made possible by the life, passion, death and resurrection of Jesus Christ, who is alive for evermore and in whom our human life is united to God.

I said just now that this new relationship is to be lived out in this life but will abide for ever. In the first chapter, when writing about the nature of our human life, I referred to the way in which man, because of his unique nature, has to hold together in one what appear to be contradictory or at least conflicting characteristics of it. He is both body and spirit. He has a personal identity and autonomy, yet is dependent upon the world and upon others. He has to live in time but also in eternity. We are already human, yet we have to become all that is implicit in being human. We see these contrasting characteristics as paradoxes.

But they are in fact complementary for the fulness of human nature, and we only see them as paradoxes because we cannot embrace the whole truth about ourselves.

As a result, we tend to oscillate. One moment, for example,

all the emphasis seems to be on personal authority. The next moment there is a swing to regard community life as all important at the expense of the individual. This is particularly so in the case of body and spirit and time and eternity. Yet it is in the body as well as in the spirit, in time, that we experience the eternal and are capable of entering into a relationship with the living God.

Because the Christian life seeks its fulfilment wholly and solely in God, it is sometimes concluded that we must adopt what Teilhard de Chardin, when warning us against it, called the minimum theory in our attitude to the created world. This means having as little to do with it as possible, seeking to escape from it into the spiritual sphere. There are passages in the New Testament which at first sight appear to support such a view. We are told that Christ came to deliver us 'from this present age of wickedness' (Gal. 1.4). St Paul tells us to 'put to death all the base pursuits of the body', and to 'give no more thought to satisfying the bodily appetite' (Rom. 8.13, 13.14). Does not our Lord himself warn us of the danger of gaining the whole world and losing our souls?

But, as Arthur McGill has said, 'The great difficulty with this kind of spiritualistic Christianity is that it confuses the "what" with the "where" of Christian love. *What* men love when they share in the divine life is God alone, with all their mind and soul and strength. If their love touches anything else, it does so in obedience to him. However, *where* they are when they love God is not in some pious ivory tower. They are in the world and not withdrawn from it. They are men of flesh and sensory perception, immersed in the concrete physical actualities of their surroundings and subjected to the concrete physical sufferings of their race.'[2] That is perfectly true but it does not really answer the point, unless we recall what Scripture says about creation. It is created by God and is essentially good, though it has 'become corrupted, for all men had lived corrupt lives on earth . . . and the earth is full of violence' (Gen. 6.12,13). However the story of the ark and the salvation of Noah proclaims the truth that creation will not be destroyed. Both the covenant with Noah and that with Moses look forward to the redemption both of man and of creation, ultimately effected in the Resurrection of Christ, the first fruits of the new creation. God does not ask us to live with him and for him in spite of having to live in the physical world, but to do so while living in it and while taking our part in its redemption and consecration. As we shall see later, the disorder of creation affects our life in Christ; yet it is as part of creation we are called so to live in it and use it that we express its praise of God. This we shall not be able to do, if we make the physical world and our physical needs and pleasure the sole object of our concern, or if we see the physical world as isolated from God its creator. We are made to love God with all our mind and soul and strength, and that includes loving what he has made in the way in which he loves it and for his sake. God loves creation for what it can become in Christ, the perfect reflection of his glory. So in the epilogue to the Bible, the Book of Revelation, where we are given a vision of creation and man redeemed in Christ, we see 'the living creatures giving glory and honour and thanks to the One who sits on the throne', and the elders acknowledging his sovereignty as they lay down their crowns before him crying, 'Thou art worthy, O Lord our God, to receive glory and honour and power because thou didst create all things; by thy will they were created, and have their being' (Rev. 4, 10.11). Then we hear 'every created thing in heaven and on earth and under the earth and in the sea, all that is in them, crying: "Praise and honour, glory and might, to him who sits on the throne and to the Lamb for ever and every!" And the four living creatues said "Amen" and the elders fell down and worshipped.'

Meanwhile the situation is as described by St Paul in his letter to the Church at Rome. 'The created universe waits with eager expectation for God's sons to be revealed. It was made the victim of frustration, not by its own choice, but because of him who made it so; yet always there was hope, because the universe itself is to be freed from the shackles of mortality and enter upon the liberty and splendour of the children of God. Up to the present, we know, the whole created universe groans in all its parts as if in the pangs of childbirth. Not only so, but we, to whom the Spirit is given as first fruits of the harvest to come, are groaning inwardly while we wait for God to make us his sons and set our whole body free.' (Rom. 8.19–23)

So it was in flesh, as part of creation that God came in Christ to share his life with men. 'But now by Christ's death in his body of flesh and blood God has reconciled you to himself, so that he may present you before himself as dedicated men, without blemish and innocent in his sight' (Col. 1.22). As Christ in his body of flesh and blood lived not only as a servant of God the Father but as the Son, offering his life of obedience with the love of the Son for the Father, so he wishes to share his life with us that we may not only be obedient servants but share his Sonship and with him say, 'Abba, Father'. So, in Ephesians, we read that 'in Christ he chose us before the world was founded, to be dedicated, to be without blemish in his sight, to be full of love; and he destined us – such was his will and pleasure – to be accepted as his sons through Jesus Christ, in order that the glory of his gracious gift, so graciously bestowed on us in his Beloved, might redound to his praise'. (Eph. 1.4–6)

How does Christ share his life with us so that we receive adoption as the children of God? As we should expect, since

God is our creator and knows what a human being is, in a way we do not, the way he has given us reflects our human nature and existence. Men and women, as we have seen, are part of creation living in and through bodies which are an integral part of their whole being. At the same time, they have unique qualities which distinguish them from the rest of creation. In the Old Testament, the human person is, before all else, a creature of God formed out the clay of the ground, but is also responsible to God, to his neighbour and for the natural world. While bodiliness meant sharing in a common humanity and sharing its nature as created by God, it also meant having a particular responsibility. In the early years of Israel's history, this was seen in corporate terms. A person's actions affected others and he shared the effect of theirs. When the recognition of personal responsibility developed, notably in the teaching of the prophet Ezekiel, the distinctiveness of the individual was seen, not so much in his separate bodily existence, defined by the boundary of his body but in the 'uniqueness of the Divine word or call to every man which demanded from him an inalterable response'.[3]

So the sharing of the life of Christ is possible in a way which takes account both of man's bodily nature and of the response which he has to make. It is effected by Baptism and by faith. By Baptism, a bodily act, we are incorporated into the body of Christ. By faith we exercise our personal responsibility of being willing to receive the gift of life in Christ from God and being prepared to accept the demands of living in Christ. (I appreciate that many are baptized in infancy, when a personal response of faith is not possible, and is made for the child by the Godparents. This is not the place to discuss the particular problem of infant Baptism, except to say first that the response of the Godparents is an essential element, and secondly that the practice does, in some sense, reflect the understanding of the Old Testament that we are not simply isolated individuals but are inextricably bound up in a common life in which we can do things for each other.)

Although a baptized person always remains baptized and cannot be re-baptized because God never fails to carry out his promises, the effect of Baptism remains dormant unless the baptized person responds and seeks to live out its meaning. Again this develops the teaching of the Old Testament, that physical membership of Israel did not by itself provide salvation, but had to be expressed in a growing obedience to the divine law. But equally, since eternal life is a gift of God, we cannot provide it ourselves. People sometimes speak of the moment when they made a conscious decision to follow Christ as the moment when they became a Christian. So to speak is to imply that becoming a Christian is something we do for ourselves and undermines the whole thrust of the Gospel which affirms that it is not the result of our merits or good works – even the merit of faith – but is the result of the action of God which we gratefully receive and to which we seek to respond.

What Jesus did in the body given to him by Mary was to be shared by those who accepted what he had done. This was to be achieved through the sacramental incorporation of men and women into his body and was to be sustained by their sacramental participation in his life through the Eucharist. Just as we do not create ourselves but are born human beings and then have to spend the rest of our lives learning to become what is meant by being human, so the new birth in Christ is given us in Baptism and we spend the rest of our lives as Christians learning to become all that we already are as Christians by grace.

As Dr Eric Mascall has written, 'The whole Catholic doctrine of the Church and of the Sacraments . . . depends upon the fact that Jesus is Man – Man triumphant, Man ascended, Man glorified but still Man. Because he is still man we are incorporated into him by our baptism. We share in his glory, our flesh is glorified.'[4] It is because our manhood is taken up into God and because we are still men and women that the manner of our incorporation and the manner of our being, nourished in our life in Christ, match the nature of our human bodily existence. In Baptism, the water of creation has to flow over us for us to be incorporated into Christ. (The natural qualities of water are also consecrated. Water in the natural order gives life. It can also drown people. In Baptism it drowns us to our benefit by drowning our old lives in Adam. It gives us the new life in Christ. It is a pity that this effective symbolism is not as evident when water is merely poured upon the candidate's head, as it is when Baptism is by immersion.) We must be physically present at the Eucharist to eat and drink so that we can be offered in Christ as members of his body and be nourished by him. The bread consecrated to be the body of the Lord is taken up to be the means by which the risen Christ, God and man, is communicated to us through the glorified humanity in which all that is created is redeemed.

It is in our bodies that we are members of Christ. It is as members of the body of Christ that we are Christians. Bishop John Robinson once wrote, 'It is almost impossible to exaggerate the materialism and crudity of Paul's doctrine of the Church as literally now the resurrection *body* of Jesus',[5] and, 'He is not saying anything so weak as that the Church is a society with a common life and governor, but that its unity is that of a single physical entity: disunion is dismemberment. For it is in fact no other than the glorified body of the risen and ascended Christ.'[6] One example of St Paul's realism is to be found in his statement, in 1 Corinthians 7.12–14, about a believing wife sanctifying her unbelieving husband so that they are both holy. On this passage Dr Schweitzer has commented, 'The unbelieving partner, through bodily connection with the believing, has a share in the latter's being-in-Christ and thereby becomes with him a member of the Community of the Sanctified. Because the married pair belong corporeally to one another, the unbelieving partner becomes, without his or her co-operation, attached to Christ and capable of receiving the powers of death and resurrection which go forth from Christ.'[7] Another example is to be found when St Paul is speaking of the way in which Christians should behave. He reminds the Christians in Corinth that some of them had lived immorally, but he then recalls their Baptism. 'But you have been through the purifying waters; you have been dedicated to God and justified through the name of the Lord Jesus and the Spirit of our God.'[8] He then asks if they have forgotten that their bodies are limbs of Christ, which should make fornication unthinkable. 'Shall I take from Christ his bodily parts and make them over to a harlot? Never!' (1 Cor. 6.15). St Paul ends positively by saying, 'Do you not know that your body is a shrine of the indwelling Holy Spirit, and the Spirit is God's gift to you? You do not belong to yourselves; you were bought at a price. Then honour God in your body.' (1 Cor. 6.19,20)

In his letter to the Christians at Rome, St Paul develops the point in another way which brings out the meaning of Baptism. 'We died to sin: how can we live in it any longer? Have you forgotten that when we were baptized into union with Christ Jesus we were baptized into his death? By baptism we were buried with him and lay dead, in order that, as Christ was raised from the dead in the splendour of the Father, so also we might set our feet upon the new path of life.' (Rom. 6.3,4). If we are to follow that new path we must first consider the nature of the Body of which we are members.

PART WITH CHRIST

GRANT me, O Lord Christ,
    growing part with thee, in thee;
        that shall not be taken away.
Part in thy purity,
    in thy courage,
        in thy peace.
Part by forgiving,
    and being forgiven.
Part in thine obedience to the Father's will,
    in thy spirit of love,
    in thy ministries of healing,
    in thy perpetual prayer.
Part in self-offering.
Part in thy sufferings,
    when it be thy call.
Part in thy victory and thy glory,
    who are GOD
        the First and the Last,
            for ever and ever.

4
The Body of Christ

During the public ministry of our Lord, his teaching was directed to revealing the characteristics and qualities of truly human life, lived as God intended. The Beatitudes, for example, are not ethical commands or instructions intended to enable men and women to achieve goodness by their own efforts. They describe the qualities of one who responds to the love of God. Our Lord reveals the innermost demands of the divine law, when it is obeyed in the spirit rather than the letter. He makes it clear that holiness depends upon trusting in God the Father with a single-minded concern to do his will. He calls men, particularly in the parables, to respond to their vocation as those created in the image of God, and to accept the challenge of being human. At the same time, particularly in his teachings of the disciples rather than the crowds, he speaks of the way in which those who followed him would live in an intimate relationship to him, rather than just obey him as a venerated teacher. So he said he was the living water to give them life; the bread of life who would nourish men with his life; the true vine of which the disciples were the branches. He said that men and women must eat his flesh and drink his blood to possess eternal life. 'As the living Father sent me, and I live because of the Father, so he who eats me shall live because of me' (St John 6.57). His words on that occasion were so direct and demanding that many of his disciples on hearing them exclaimed, 'This is more than we can stomach! Why listen to such talk?' and 'many of the disciples withdrew and no longer went about with him'.

On the night before he was betrayed, he instituted the Eucharist, anticipating his resurrection by which, in and through his body, creation would be liberated so that it wholly expressed God's design. After Pentecost, when men and women would bring bread 'which earth has given and human hands have made' and wine, 'fruit of the vine and work of human hands', and place them in the Lord's hand, then by the energizing of the Spirit, they would become the means by which the life of his risen body would be communicated to his body, the Church. In the Epistles the description of the Church as the body of Christ predominates over all other descriptions such as the household of God, a royal priesthood, the people of God. It is called the temple of the Holy Spirit because it is the body of Christ, just as when our Lord spoke of himself as the temple which would be destroyed but which would be raised again in three days, he did so because he 'was speaking of his body'. It is the temple because God dwells in Christ in whom the perfect worship of sacrifice is offered and the reconciliation of man with God which is the purpose of sacrifice is achieved.

When we consider how we should live as members of the body of Christ the first fact we need to remember is that 'Christ is like a single body with its many limbs and organs, which, many as they are, together make up one body. For indeed we were all brought into one body by baptism in the one Spirit whether we are Jews or Greeks, whether slaves or free men' (1 Cor. 12.12-13); and 'just as in a single human body there are many limbs and organs, all with different functions, so all of us, united with Christ, form one body, serving individually as limbs and organs to one another'. (Rom. 12.4)

St Paul develops this truth simply but graphically in 1 Corinthians. 'A body is not one single organ, but many.

Suppose the foot should say, "Because I am not a hand, I do not belong to the body", it does belong to the body none the less. Suppose the ear were to say, "Because I am not an eye, I do not belong to the body", it does still belong to the body. If the body were all eye, how could it hear? If the body were all ear, how could it smell? But, in fact, God appointed each limb and organ to its own place, as he chose. If the whole were one single organ, there would not be a body at all; in fact, however, there are many different organs, but one body. The eye cannot say to the hand, "I do not need you"; nor the head to the feet, "I do not need you". Quite the contrary: those organs of the body which seem to be more frail than others are indispensable, and those parts of the body which we regard as less honourable are treated with special honour. To our unseemly parts is given a more than ordinary seemliness, whereas our seemly parts need no adorning. But God has combined the various parts of the body, giving special honour to the humbler parts, so that there might be no sense of division in the body, but that all its organs might feel the same concern for one another. If one organ suffers, they all suffer together. If one flourishes, they all rejoice together.' (1 Cor. 12.14–26)

I have pointed out elsewhere that modern medicine enables us to see another truth implicit in the analogy of a human body. A healthy organism functions in the way St Paul describes. Take a cross-section of it and a structured pattern of differentiated cells is revealed, each cell performing its proper functions. But if you take a cross-section of a cancerous growth, what is revealed is a multiplicity of identical cells, one cell having run wild and reproduced itself at the expense of the body. In the Church as the body of Christ, self-centredness is not only destructive of the individual, it is also destructive of the Church as a body. This analogy is developed in a most illuminating way by the missionary doctor, Paul Brand, who, in two recent books,[1] uses his knowledge of the functions of the human body to express the meaning of the fact that the Church is the body of Christ.

On the particular point which I mentioned above he begins, in a chapter entitled 'Mutiny', by describing the condition of a Madras woman, a beggar, who was suffering from a massive lipoma, a tumour of fat cells. Her condition arose from the fact that, as he puts, it 'the (fat) cells function beautifully except for one flaw – they have become disloyal. In their activity they disregard the body's needs. And so the beggar woman in Madras gradually starved while a lipoma that was part of her engorged itself.'

This analogy from nature should remind us that as Christians we should resist the modern idea that for people to be equal they must be identical and perform identical functions. What matters, as St Paul makes so clear, is that each member of the body of Christ, like individual cells in a human body, carries out his or her own vocation for the sake of the whole body of which Christ is the head, whose authority is loyally accepted, and does not seek to be envious of those with other vocations or seek to do their job. To live as a Christian is to carry out a particular role as an integral part of a living organism. Too often, Christians regard the Church as an institution which they support or to which they look for help. Of course, membership of the Church involves an obligation to support it. Very early in the life of the Church St Paul organized a relief fund to support the poor Christians in Jerusalem. He urges support for the widows in the Church and presses for a proper stipend for the presbyters (and a double stipend for the presbyters who do well). He bases what he says upon the responsibility which all members have for the common life of the body. He does not speak as if it were an institution worthy of support like a society for meeting a particular need in society which well-intentioned citizens would do well to help. No one would want to deny that the Church is to serve those who need help. It is the servant Church with the vocation to serve humanity. But it can only offer the help it should, namely the re-creation of men and women, if it is true to its nature because such help is given by their incorporation into its very life. What really matters is that Christians see the Church as the body of which they are living members, not as an organization outside themselves, to which they can attach or detach themselves at will. Still less should they identify the Church with the clergy or with those who carry out its administration.

If we are going to have a proper understanding of the Church which is still in space and time – 'the Church militant here in earth', we must also remember that it is but part of the body of Christ, which exists in space and time, but transcends both. That part of the Church which is still on earth is by far the smallest part. Christian tradition has spoken of three phases or states of the Church's existence – the Church militant, the Church expectant and the Church triumphant. These names are not to be found in the Scriptures but they reflect and express what the Scriptures say about the Church. St Paul speaks of those who have died but are alive in Christ and who no longer have to live by faith. They look forward with serenity and confidence to the consummation of all things at the end of the ages. In the Book of Revelation, we are given a dramatic vision of the fulfilment of the universe by its consecration to God in Christ and its transfiguration so that it perfectly reflects back the glory of God to him in perfect love.

We live as members of the body of Christ with all who have been incorporated into him on earth, but not only with them.

We are fellow members with all God's people with the Blessed Virgin Mary, the apostles, martyrs, doctors and confessors, from whose prayers we benefit, as we benefit from those of Christians on earth. They constantly remind us of our vocation and of our true destiny. Many through their writings speak to us today. I remember vividly how, at an Anglican-Orthodox theological discussion, one Greek archbishop, when referring to something he had read in the works of Maximus the Confessor, a theologian of the sixth century who united theology and spirituality in a marvellous way, did so in these words, 'Only last week, Maximus the Confessor was saying to me'. For the archbishop, Maximus was alive in Christ, not merely a very saintly man who lived some thirteen hundred years ago.

What then is our vocation as members of Christ? Vocation is a word which, in common use in the Church, is restricted to those who are called to the priesthood, the diaconate or some other accredited ministry in the Church. In the world it is used largely of those in particular caring professions or occupations, such as doctors, nurses or teachers. It is, in fact, a word which applies to every Christian. We are all called by God. The initiative is his. Not only our baptism and our faith but our whole Christian life is a response to his call. All of us, by our incorporation into the body of him who is eternally God and man, are called to allow his glorified humanity to be lived in us and, through him and in him, to live in communion with God. We have to do so with the temperament and talents with which we have been created, rejoicing to allow them to be consecrated to God in his service and to his glory.

The vocation of each one of us is primarily to be fulfilled in our ordinary daily life, in our work, our family life, our leisure and in our relationships to our neighbours. Too often, at the present day, the impression is given that the authentic

Christian is one who is engaged in 'church work', such as being a member of a parochial church council or a synod, organizing a conference, or taking part in some voluntary social activity in the name of the Church. For some people, doing such things is part of their vocation, and we must be grateful to those who respond to the call to take part in the necessary organization and administration of the life of the Church. But we must never imagine that only they are engaged in 'church work' and that it is simply the duty of the ordinary Christian to support them. The real work of the Church is done by ordinary Christians in their ordinary lives, and the job of those who can and should be engaged in the domestic affairs of the Church is to enable them to do it better. Commitments outside the home are for the majority of Christians likely to be visiting the sick and housebound, shopping for the elderly, and providing listening ears for those who are depressed or in personal difficulties, rather than attending the PCC or a conference on the 'place of the laity'.

How are we to fulfil our vocation? In the Epistles in the New Testament, we find that Christians are described by what has happened to them at God's hands. So we read that they are 'sanctified by Christ', or 'justified by Christ'. As a result we are 'in Christ', and this is contrasted with the fact that just as human beings we are 'in Adam'. As we possess our human life by being born as members of mankind, so by grace we possess our Christian life by the fact that we are reborn as members of the new humanity in Christ. We also find that we are described as being 'in the Lord', and there is an important difference between the meaning of the two phrases. This difference is related to the way in which the titles of Christ and Lord are used. Generally speaking, when the title 'Christ' is used, it is in the context of indicating what

God has done for us and what we *are* in Christ by grace, whereas the title 'Lord' is used in the context of indicating what we should become if we are truly to live in Christ. Professor Moule sums it up by saying that the difference means 'Become, *in the Lord*, what you already are *in Christ*'.[2] In other words we fulfil our vocation, given to us in Christ, by learning to accept the will of Christ as our sovereign Lord.

How then do we discern his will? What we have to realize is made clear to us by St Paul at the beginning of the twelfth chapter of his letter to the Romans. He begins, 'Therefore, my brothers, I implore you by God's mercy to offer your very selves to him: a living sacrifice, dedicated and fit for his acceptance, for such is the worship which you, as rational creatures, should offer. Adapt yourselves no longer to the pattern of this present world, but let your minds be remade and your whole nature thus transformed'. At this point, it might be expected that he would go on to say that if we so live, we shall do so to the glory of God or the praise of the glory of his grace. In fact, he continues, 'Then you will be able to discern the will of God, and to know what is good, acceptable, and perfect'. In other words, if we are to be able to know what is involved in accepting Christ as Lord, we must first set our wills to obey him. This may seem paradoxical, even unreasonable, but it is not unlike what we have to do in the case of other simple activities, such as learning to swim or to ride a bicycle. It is impossible to learn to swim until we are willing to take our feet off the bottom and commit ourselves to swimming, or to learn to ride a bicycle until we have put both our feet on the pedals and tried to set off. No amount of theoretical learning or practice of the necessary motions will avail us until we do so. In the case of obeying Christ, another factor also operates. Trust is essential and he has given us reason to trust him by dying and rising again. By his resurrection, he demonstrates that he who puts his trust in God is not confounded. We shall not discover what his will is, or we shall distort it to meet our own desires, if we try to discover what it is before we decide whether or not we want to obey him.

Blind obedience, however, is not what he asks for. It is the worship of mind and heart, the worship as rational creatures, we should offer. It is for this reason that we shall consider what this means in terms of our minds, hearts and bodies. But, at this stage, I want to make another point. The way in which we are guided to discern the will of the Lord when we set out to obey him is not unlike one method of direction-finding which was used by aircraft. The navigator flew between two beams, each of which emitted pulses. By keeping the pulses from each in balance, he was able to direct the aircraft on its desired course. As Christians we have two beams, the one coming from the Scriptures, with their record of what God has done in Christ. This beam represents the historical element in the Christian faith and the fact that the Gospel does not derive from the speculations of men but from what God has done. The other beam comes from the use of our minds, our hearts and our bodies. The Holy Spirit guides us, as it were, as we listen to both beams. He enables us to hear the true meaning of Scripture and he enables us to use our minds, hearts and bodies for God, and to relate properly what we hear from both beams. If we attempt to use Scripture as a kind of rule book in a literal way, which takes no account of what men have come to know by the exercise of their God-given talents and skills, we shall go off course. Likewise, if we disregard the Scriptures or attempt to modify their essential message to suit contemporary thought, rather than to bring it under the judgment of Scripture, we shall find that we are simply obeying our own desires.

HOLY CHURCH

LORD GOD, thou hast built in heaven and earth
    a single Church
 of Truth and Love and holy Spirit;
one family and communion, whose temple is the Lamb,
one body indivisible, here and beyond,
    the Body of thy dear Son.

Thou art its foundation and corner-stone, thou its head
    and life,
    O JESUS EMMANUEL;
thou, whom we have seen and touched and know,
  eternal Truth, eternal Love, holy and eternal Spirit.

Who is like GOD? Does GOD build upon the sand?
  Against God's mind, against God's Church,
    what can prevail?
Who can contract its bounds? who divide the Divine?
  Not mortal men on its temporal fringes,
    not we who crucify Christ.

The unity of holy Church, its might, its gospel
  proceeding each from GOD's unalterable will,
    is Truth and Love and holy Spirit.
Its ministries, O GOD, stream from thy heart,
  Truth, Love, and holy Spirit, one and all.
There is no other Truth than thine, nor can be such a Love,
and all made ours within one family, one Father's House,
  one Vine, one Bread and Cup, one Body.

Father, all souls are thine: gather them into one;
  bring us into the one Truth;
  bind us by the one Love;
  perfect us with the one Spirit;

pity our senile schisms, heal the long hates of death;
within they single Church built of thy grace,
    grant us thy peace.

5

The Mind of a Christian

As I tried to make clear in the first chapter, the ability to reflect upon the meaning of life, to discern the pattern and structure of the created world and to make conscious and deliberate decisions based upon such reflection and discernment is one of the distinctive characteristics of the human person. In what sense is this to be fulfilled in the Christian life? In answering that question we have to be very careful. On the one hand, since that ability as a human characteristic is found to some degree in every person, it must form an essential element in the life of every Christian. On the other hand, it would be contrary to the Gospel and destructive of it, if intellectual abilities of a particular order were made a requirement of living an authentic Christian life. The Gospel is for everyone, of whatever ability or temperament, and it would be fatal to suggest that only those with a university degree in theology could be proper Christians. The same danger lies in respect of the heart and body. Some people are naturally more religious by temperament than others. Authentic Christian living must not be limited to those who are capable of certain feelings or sensibilities. Likewise, it must not be limited to those to whom an ascetic and highly ordered life is natural and attractive.

Nevertheless, Christians, as human beings, have minds and must think about their faith. I say, 'think about their faith', because while we have to use our minds, we must not imagine that the Christian faith is something which we work out for ourselves. Thinking about it must be a response to what God has revealed to us about himself. When St John is speaking about the apostolic preaching, he says, 'What we have seen and heard we declare to you, so that you and we together may share in a common life, that life which we share with the Father and his Son Jesus Christ.' (1 John 1.3). St Paul in his first letter to Timothy distinguishes between 'mere speculation' and 'God's plan' which he has made known to us'.

The Bible is, above all, the record of the acts of God. It is as a result of those acts that we live as Christians today. The Church sprang from those acts and its life must express and be in accord with their meaning. It is for this reason that the Scriptures have always been seen as the touchstone of the expression of the faith in successive generations. We have on the one hand to be sensitive to the guidance of the Holy Spirit who enables us to see the meaning of the faith for our times; and, on the other hand, have to be faithful to the revelation which we have received. It is very easy to identify what we want or what is congenial to our generation with the guidance of the Holy Spirit. That is why we need the touchstone of Scripture. But Scripture is not a rule-book which is to be applied mechanically, without taking account of the immense changes which have taken place in human life since the first AD. How then are we to use the Scriptures, both as we read them and listen to what they say to us, and as we use them to test our thinking about the faith?

Living as we do in the second half of the twentieth century, we have to ask this question in the light of what is called 'higher criticism', that is, the meticulous study of the biblical texts in the light of newly discovered documents, archaeological finds, and new knowledge about the times in which the documents were written. One effect of such criticism since the middle of the last century, has been the questioning of the authority of Scripture. Before I discuss this effect, I must point out that the assumption which is often made, that biblical criticism only began in the nineteenth century, is mistaken. J.K. Mozley wrote in 1936:

> It is, of course, a quite unscientific simplification of the issue when it is supposed that before the rise of the 'Higher Criticism' there was no such thing as Biblical criticism. For some of the problems, both in the textual and in the literary sphere, were patent, and some examination of them, with a result following thereon, was unavoidable. Origen in the third century was well acquainted with problems as to the true text of Scripture – that is, as to what the author of a particular book had actually written. Augustine a century and more later knew that an explanation was needed of the close resemblances often to be found in the texts of St Matthew and St Mark. His solution, that Mark was follower and abbreviator of Matthew, is one that a great number of scholars today would find it necessary to reject, but it is a critical solution. No one could think of Colet and Erasmus as other than "critics" in their attitude to Scripture, while Luther, as is well known, did not hesitate to bring to the evaluation of the various books in the Bible the criterion of whether or not he found Christ preached therein.[1]

The disciplined use of the mind in critical scholarship is a necessary and proper activity. God chose to act in a particular way at a particular moment in history. The record of what he did was set down by men who, though inspired by the Holy Spirit, were fallible men of their time, living in a culture which is very different from that of today. The record was produced over a long period of time and, in the case of both Old and

New Testaments, what was recorded was the experience of men as they lived under the impact of the events within a community which had been brought into being by them.

The Bible came into being, not because men set out to write an ancient history, though it contains history, or a book of spiritual and moral teachings, though they too are to be found in it. The Bible was written because men believed that from the time of Abraham until Pentecost, God has acted in history in events which were of eternal significance for mankind, first in the formation of the Israelites as the people of God, and then supremely in Christ, through whom and in whom the New Israel, the Church, of which they were members, came into being. The Christian Church took over the Old Testament, as it came to be recognized as authoritative by the Jews. The Church also recognized as authoritative the documents which now comprise the New Testament.

What is known as the 'Canon' of the New Testament came into being, that is, the list of those writings which were recognized as having unique authority for the Church as it sought to live in the light of the events of the Gospel. The process, which was completed in the fourth century, took place side by side with the development of the creeds, which summarized the biblical understanding of God, of the relationship of the world to him, and of human life. Both Scriptures and creeds came into being as the Church sought to ensure that in its continuing life biblical and credal understanding would be normative. In other words, while witnessing to the historical events which brought the Church into being, it distilled the essential meaning of those events, so that they would speak of God's revelation to future generations and would also serve as a text by which they could determine whether the expression of the Gospel in different times and different cultures was faithful to that revelation.

To live with the mind of a Christian is to be committed to that biblical understanding of which the Old Testament speaks and which was perfectly expressed in the mind of Christ. To say that is not to ask for a blind and irrational act of faith; it is to recognize the essential basis of belief which is involved in professing the Christian faith. Many of the acute problems for the Church today arise from the fact that, as Bishop Lesslie Newbigin has put in his brilliant little book *The Other Side of 1984*, the critical study of the Bible – and I would add, attempts to understand and re-express the faith – have for two centuries been conducted in the context of an understanding of reality and life which is not that of the Bible. It is sometimes evident, for example, that objections are raised by theologians and biblical scholars to the Gospel narratives and their plain meaning, not because of difficulties in the accounts themselves, but because what they are seeking to convey does not accord with assumptions derived from elsewhere than the Scriptures. If this be so, then the proper course is for such scholars to admit openly that their objections are essentially to the underlying belief of the biblical writers and to argue against them, rather than to allow the impression to be given that they spring simply from a 'scientific' examination of the documents.

The assumptions with which not only scholars but many thinking Christians approach the Bible and the Christian faith today often spring from the thought of the eighteenth century in what is known as the Enlightenment. It is remarkable that in the last few years, it has become increasingly recognized in many areas of thought, such as politics and art, how much our approach has been dominated by the Enlightenment. This has led to a questioning of its assumptions,[2] which put man in the centre of the world. These assumptions laid great stress upon reason, observation and experiment, by which he could discern the facts about the universe. Facts were regarded as creating or revealing their own meaning, and man could thereby possess a true understanding of reality. It followed that as neutral an approach to the facts as possible was regarded as desirable, and such an approach was alone regarded as deserving the title 'scientific'. Such is the popular understanding of the word 'scientific' today, with the consequent belief that only that which is measurable is real, and that all other knowledge is subjective, expressing no more than the hopes and fears of men and women with no basis in reality.

In practice, such a neutral approach is impossible. In the first place, those who adopt it make certain unprovable assumptions about the nature of reality and life. Secondly, the scientific developments of particularly the last sixty years have made evident the inadequacy of the Newtonian physics which undergirded the approach of the Enlightenment. Today scientists speak in very different terms about, for example, 'mass' and 'energy' from the way they did a hundred years ago, and it is recognized that the facts about mass and energy have not changed, but man's understanding of them and his attempts to express the reality about them have. It is increasingly recognized that our attempts to express reality are, in a sense, always provisional and that reality stands over against us and judges our attempts to be grasped by it and understand it.

Any study or research, whether it be in science, history or theology, starts from an intuition, the acceptance of a tradition or an act of faith, on the basis of which the facts selected for examination are chosen. The facts are then used to check the underlying theory of hypothesis. But to select the facts or then examine them, on a basis which is inappropriate and which does not accord with their nature, is to ask for trouble. The examination of any organism or instrument must be on the basis of the purpose for which it is designed. The consideration of any person must be on the basis of what he or she professes to be and hopes to achieve. If we examine them on the basis of what we think they ought to be, our study will not reveal the truth about them.

As far as the Bible is concerned, it was designed to enable us to hear and to respond to the revelation of God. We must apply our minds to the study of Scripture, but we must study it for what it is, not what we would like it to be. The Bible, and the Gospels in particular, were not written simply as a record to aid remembrance, but as the means by which the Church could enter into and live by the meaning of the events of man's redemption. These took place in a particular culture at a particular time. Biblical scholars must ask what is the significance of the fact that God chose that particular place and moment. This requires examination of the background against which the authors wrote and the meaning of the thought-forms they used. They must also ask what the Church sought to preserve as it recognized the books of Scripture as possessing unique authority, so that the Church in subsequent generations would be faithful to the significance of the acts which brought it into being. For this reason, as Professor R.E. Brown has said, 'Biblical hermeneutics, or the search for the meaning of Scripture, cannot be content with the literal sense (the meaning that a book had when it was first composed); it must look for the meaning that the book had when it became scriptural or part of the Bible, i.e. part of the Canon'.[3] What is not legitimate for a biblical scholar is to adopt an approach which is contrary to the main purpose and thrust of Scripture and then to reject the content of Scripture because it does not agree with that approach. To take one example: Scripture assumes and proclaims that God is sovereign Lord, who, while respecting the freedom which he has given to man, can and does intervene in the affairs of the world and of men. To seek to interpret Scripture on the assumption that he does not intervene but merely set the world going like a clock, leaving it to run its course, will mean that much of Scripture will be unacceptable and will be explained away.

To profess the Christian faith is to commit oneself to living in the revelation of which the Bible is a record, learning to see how it affects our understanding of God, man and the world. The Bible must not be used as source book to support our own ideas. We must listen to it, with all the help the biblical scholars can give us, as the word of God which is 'living and active', and which is 'sharper than any two-edged sword, piercing to the division of soul and spirit, of joints and marrow, and discerning the thoughts and intentions of the heart.' (Heb. 4.12–13 RSV).

As Sir Edwyn Hoskyns wrote, 'The Church does not require of us that we should master a new vocabulary but that we should apprehend the meaning of the commonest words in our language: it demands that we should not at the critical moment turn away from the meaning of words but that we should wrestle with them and refuse to let them go. For from these common words, from 'life' and 'death', from 'good' and 'evil', from 'judgement' and 'mercy', there peers out at us from our quite ordinary life, from the world of men and of things, a secret which concerns us and from which we cannot escape'. That secret is revealed through Scripture. It is the secret that life comes through death – death to our self-centredness by the power of the cross, to a resurrection in Christ and new life in him. It is the secret which Scripture proclaims as the key to all life.

When I say the Apostles Creed in worship, I am committing myself to the biblical view of life which it expresses. I am committing myself to God as the creator of all things; to God who acts in human history; supremely in Christ, to God who is my judge and my saviour; to God who wills that I should live with him in Christ beyond space and time. The creed witnesses to the fact that God, Father, Son and Holy Spirit, reveals himself as the blessed Trinity of love, who is reality. The meaning of the creed transcends my understanding, for it seeks to put into human words the truth about God, who surpasses our knowledge. When I say the creed I am expressing my faith into which I hope to grow. The question I ask is not, 'How can I adapt the creed to fit my understanding?' but 'How can I by worship, prayer, meditating upon the Scriptures and the use of my reason, learn in obedience to love and know more truly the eternal reality of whom it speaks?' When I say the Nicene Creed in the Eucharist I share in the positive affirmation of belief of the Church which was hammered out to exclude certain false opinions which were seen to be incompatible with God's revelation of himself.

The use of his mind by a Christian has first to be exercised by allowing it to be grasped by the meaning of the professed faith of the Church. Side by side with that, he has to seek to apply his understanding of that faith to the situation in which he finds himself and to the decisions he has to make. In so doing he has to take account of a distinction which is firmly set in the Anglican tradition, namely the distinction between doctrine which is necessary for salvation, and opinions on which it is legitimate for Christians to differ. There are matters on which, with faithfulness to the biblical tradition, Christians can properly differ as to the appropriate policy to be pursued. This is particularly important at the present time when endorsement of a particular policy on a contemporary issue is often made the criterion of committed Christian discipleship.

How then should a Christian use the Scripture? It may seem obvious, but it is first necessary to stress the need to read them and to read them as a whole. Simply to listen to the necessarily brief passages which are selected for use in public worship, whether in the Eucharist or in the Offices, is not sufficient. The systematic reading of individual books is essential and the question we should be asking ourselves when we do so is, 'What has this book to say about the catholic and apostolic faith which led the Church to include it in the Canons of Scripture?' To help us to answer that question we need to draw on the wisdom of the Church as it lives in the tradition. There is an urgent need for parish priests to expound Scripture in a way which serves to answer this question. We can also use commentaries and a number are suggested in the list of suggested further reading. What we must not do is to make up our minds about what we think the Faith should be and then look up the passages in Scripture to support our views. The use of isolated texts to 'prove' certain points has in the past been associated with a fundamentalist view of the Scriptures, which interpreted them literally in a way which ignored their historical origins and the purpose for which they were recognized as authoritative. Such use is, however, to be found today in support of particular causes, such as liberation theology, or feminism, and is as a illegitimate a use of Scripture, as is the other. Both spring from the adoption of a particular standpoint which does not accord with that of Scripture as a whole. The first springs from a failure to take seriously the fact that God acts in history, treating his agents not as puppets but as rational human beings living at a particular time. The second seeks to impose a framework of thought which is not that of the Bible as the basis of its interpretation, and subjects it to the judgment of contemporary thought of each succeeding fashion.

There is one book which really does help us to see how the Bible speaks about the fundamental issues of human life and our relationship to God. That is *Reflections on the Psalms* by C.S. Lewis which, although primarily concerned with the Psalms, illuminates our understanding of the Bible as a whole. This is not surprising since the Psalms have spoken in a unique way to mean and women of all times.

To have the mind of a Christian is not merely to think about the faith or so-called religious beliefs. It is to see the whole of life in the context of the faith. It is to embrace the whole of life, seeing it in the context of man's eternal destiny as the redeemed child of God. As Harry Blamires has written: 'You can think christianly or you can think secularly about the most sacred things – the sacrament of the altar, for example. Likewise you can think christianly or you can think secularly about the most mundane objects – say, about a petrol pump . . . . There is nothing in our experience, however trivial, worldly or even evil, which cannot be thought about christianly. There is likewise nothing in our experience which cannot be thought about secularly – considered, that is to say, simply in its relationship to the passing existence of bodies and psyches in a time-locked universe'.[5]

The secular mind assumes that this world constitutes the whole of reality and that human existence does not continue beyond death. If religion is recognized, it is seen as one means devised by man to make this life more tolerable but is given no ultimate significance. Secondly, it denies the reality of human freedom to choose between love and hate, good and evil, justice and injustice. Man is regarded as being at the mercy of his upbringing or environment, or of psychological pressures within himself. As a result, he is seen as suffering from permanently diminished responsibility, or as having none at all. Not only are his actions excusable; manipulation, sanctions, and social pressure are justified, being seen as methods to make him behave better, and unjustifiable hope is placed in the power of legislation or planning to improve him. Another characteristic of the secular mind is that it regards suffering as the worst evil and that anything is justified if it appears to relieve suffering, even if it is morally wrong or involves the acceptance of what is morally wrong. Ironically, at the same time, the secular mind has inherited the belief of the Enlightenment that obedience to authority outside itself is an affront to human dignity, and for this reason rejected belief in God, as it was rightly seen as recognizing man's dependence upon God and upon his neighbour.

The mind of the Christian, by contrast, sees all life with an eternal perspective, recognizing that the one thing which matters more than anything else is our relationship to God, a relationship which has first to be lived in time but which abides through death and beyond. In this life, man, if he is to be truly human, must learn how he can grow into his true self and into reality, by allowing what is of God to take shape and be embodied in him. The Christian believes that man is created in the image of God, with the privilege of loving God and his neighbours. This ability to love means that man has an inner freedom, however much his circumstances may restrict it, for love must by its very nature be freely willed. No one can compel someone to love. This is seen on the cross, where God redeems us in a way which still leaves us free to choose. While free, we have to face the consequences of the choices we make and those of the choices of others. Human freedom is one reason why we have to face suffering. To try to evade suffering is to deny human freedom. The Gospel is the perfect example of love accepting the cost of loving. Our Lord suffers because when faced with the consequence of man's sin, he suffers rather than disobey the Father in an attempt to evade it.

Above all, the Christian knows that, because man is made for love, acceptance of dependence upon God and upon our fellow citizens of earth is the only way to be free to become our true selves. To deny our dependence in the interests of a self-centred autonomy is ultimately to isolate ourselves completely, which is hell. Likewise, to deny our freedom and our responsibility, on the grounds that all our actions are excusable because they are determined by factors outside our control, is to reduce ourselves to a condition which is less than human.

In most of his letters St Paul begins by an exposition of what God has done in Christ by which man has been liberated to love God. He then comes to the point where he uses some such phrase as, 'Wherefore, for this cause', that is, because of what God has done and because of what you are by grace, this is the way you should now live. In other words, Christian behaviour derives from what we are. The way to develop a Christian mind is to allow ourselves to be grasped by the meaning of the faith as it expresses the divine action, a process which will not or should not end until we die. St Paul, in his letter to the Philippians, in words which paralled those in Romans 12 which have already been quoted in the context of our membership of the body of Christ, tells us to have the mind of Christ. Having then spoken of Our Lord's incarnation, death and exaltation, he says 'So you too, my friends, must be obedient as always . . . You must work out your own salvation in fear and trembling; for it is God who works in you, inspiring both the will and the deed, for his own chosen purpose'. (Phil. 2.12–13).

IN CHRIST

CHRIST be in me,
>   the hope of glory;
> for joy, for peace,
> for love, for life,
>   for death to self.

CHRIST be in me
>   to purge my sin
>   and heal mine infirmities:
> to open mine eyes on the deep things of God
>   on new worlds of truth
>   and new heavens of love,
>   freely given.

CHRIST be in me
>   to fight the old man
>   and mould the new;
> to constrain my thinking, speaking, and doing
>   by his Spirit of strength,
>   by his Spirit of gentleness;
> CHRIST my defence against all mine enemies,
>   CHRIST my victory.

O CHRIST, Light of God, light of men,
>   dwell in my heart by faith,
>   dwell in my mind,
>   dwell in my whole being
>   to build there thine own image;
> until the likeness be nearer like,
>   and my life hid with THINE
>   IN GOD

6

The Body of a Christian

The Christian is called to live in Christ as a human being, which means that he has to do so in his body of flesh and blood. It is in and through the body that he is baptized into Christ and shares his life in Holy Communion. It is also in and through man's body that he has to live as a member of the body of Christ.

The Christian faith is essentially sacramental; but this is often taken to mean no more than that God gives us grace and nourishes our spiritual life through the Sacraments. The Christian life is understood as something which happens in the mind, at times with the impression that in some mysterious way the mind can operate apart from the body. When, by way of reaction, place is given in Christian worship to the body, as for example in dance or mime, the body is sometimes used in a way which simply affirms it, without discerning how it is to be consecrated and related to soul and mind. The history of the Church has been marred on occasion by the false teaching that, if we have faith, we can do what we like with our bodies, an error which St Paul refutes in Romans 6. Generally speaking, the impression has been given that the body is dangerous, and what is experienced in and through the body is to be regarded with suspicion. It is not surprising that Christians have acquired a reputation for being life-rejecting rather than life-affirming.

The fact that our bodily condition can and does affect our spiritual condition is not sufficient to account for this situation. The reverse is also true. Our bodily achievements are affected by our mental attitude, just as bodily suffering can be used as the means of spiritual discipline and renewal. The fact is that both mind and body are capable of being the spheres of spiritual health by consecration to God in Christ, and both are capable of being misused and of manifesting the effects of misuse.

What are the characteristics of the human body? I do not mean characteristics in terms of its physical nature, which in its complexity and operation is quite astounding: I mean its characteristics in relation to ourselves. In the first place, the body is the means by which we act. This is obvious in terms of the physical actions we need to perform in order to exist, such as eating, drinking, earning our living and so on. It is also indispensable for the exercise of the skills of the artist, the poet, the surgeon, the musician. Man has been described as 'an animated implement – a spirit that possesses and animates its tool from within and truly expresses itself in the very action from within'.[1] The same is true of what we describe as our spiritual activities. To pray involves a mental act which requires the activity of a brain, as does the intention to act with a particular motive or, say, love or compassion.

Secondly, to use the body for action involves learning and discipline. In the case of a new-born baby they are necessary even for the basic acts of feeding and walking. Learning and discipline are necessary not merely for one part, say, one hand or one eye. The members of the body have to be co-ordinated and operate as parts of a single body. What is true of a baby is true in another way of the artist, the musician, the craftsman. Visions of beauty do not in themselves create the ability to achieve them. What they do is to give the will to discipline the body, in order that the skill may be acquired for them to be achieved.

For, thirdly, it is through the body that we are able to

express ourselves; through our words, our gestures, our looks we communicate what we are. It is through the body that the life of society is possible, for it is through our body that we become aware of others and can relate to them. Even when, in the case of those who know each other at the deepest level, there is a kind of intuitive awareness, it is mediated through the body.

It is also through the body that we are able to allow our souls to speak of God and communicate his love. That is the function of the body of a saint and, in that case, the body can be so much at the disposal of God that it becomes transparent to his glory. The face of a holy person, though in the accepted sense not a beautiful one, can become luminous with a serenity and love which bestow beauty upon it.

It is in the body that we experience emotion, sometimes with a frightening intensity which can take us unawares. The problem is that though we know that to experience such emotions is necessary if we are to experience the depths of human experience, we do not want to be at their mercy. To be overwhelmed by our emotions can give a sense of shame at having lost control of ourselves. This is understandable if the emotion be one which we know to be wrong, such as hatred, but it can also happen when we know that the emotion is one which is good.

I spoke earlier of the fact that we express ourselves through our bodies. That is true of all our relationships, even the most casual, and we must not minimize its importance. Even an accidental collision in a crowded street can be used as the means for expressing the love of God in love for our neighbour, rather than of resentment or disrespect. But the supreme dignity of the human body is that it is the means by which we enter into communion with another person and procreate life.

At the same time, the body does present particular problems and dangers. So, of course, does the mind. Intellectual arrogance, for example, which can corrupt the mind, is a subtle sin which can masquerade as a concern for truth and influence us while we are still unconscious of it. The sins of the mind come from the undisciplined exercise of one of man's highest qualities – his ability to reason, but they do not press upon us with the insistence and the immediate satisfaction of those of the body. The sins of the body spring from its abandonment of reason, for they represent the triumph of the irrational. Whether it be intoxication by alcohol, by drugs, by sexuality, their satisfaction involves the deliverance of man into forces beyond his control. They involve imprisonment to a kind of inexorable determinism.

Yet the desire for physical ecstacy is a reflection of the fact that the body is, though fallen like the rest of our human nature, created by God and is to have its place in redeemed humanity. In other words, living as a Christian does not involve so controlling and disciplining our bodies that our spiritual life can survive and grow in spite of them. Our bodies are not simply the vehicles in which we are enabled to live our spiritual life. That life, the life of the soul, has to be lived in and through our bodies. Holiness involves both our bodies and our minds, just as sin can involve both. This truth has been obscured by the translation in the Authorized Version which contrasts the 'works of the flesh' and the 'fruits of the Spirit'. When St Paul uses the word 'flesh', he is not referring to the body as opposed to the mind. He uses the word 'flesh' to describe the whole of human nature when it is subject to the rule of sin. By contrast, life in the Spirit means the consecration of the whole of our being to God. The true distinction is also confused by the regrettable translation in the Good News Bible of the word *sarx*, for which 'flesh' is used in the Authorized Version, by the words 'human nature'. The true distinction which we have to make is made clear in the accurate translation in the New English Bible of *sarx* as 'lower nature'. It is that 'lower nature', not human nature as such, which 'sets its desires against the Spirit'. That this is the true meaning of what St Paul says is confirmed by the fact that, in his list of sins, he includes both sins of the mind as well as those of the body: 'fornication, impurity and indecency; idolatry and sorcery; quarrels, a contentious temper, envy, fits of rage, selfish ambitions, dissension, party intrigues and jealousies; drinking bouts, orgies and the like'.

However, the qualities of our human bodies are not merely to be used in the service of God. It is in and through our bodies as well as our minds that we are able to experience God and his activities in creation. Body and mind are both inextricably interwoven as constituent elements in the human nature with which we live as human beings. G.L. Prestige in his life of Bishop Charles Gore gives an example of the experience of mind expressed in the body. He recalls how Gore was once seen on the stairs hugging to his breast a volume of Hastings' *Encyclopaedia of Religion and Ethics*. 'His eyes beamed in an ecstasy of intellectual joy', and when asked the cause of this transfiguration, he said, 'A.E. Taylor's article on God – entitled "Theism" '.[2]

What matters is that the experience in our bodies is recognized as having its source in God. Only when that is so, will it be a means of our knowing God and be consecrated to his glory. Before considering some of the various ways in which we experience God in and through our bodies, two points must be borne in mind.

First, the activities of God in his loving relationship towards us can never be divided into those which are sacred and those which are secular. While it is true that, in the

Sacraments, God acts in a special way – the way of promise or covenant upon which we can rely, his action in the Sacraments is part of his continuing and unified self-giving of himself in love to his creation, and the grace given in the Sacrament is for the whole of human life, not just a religious part of it.

Secondly, while we do have a real experience of the divine energies through our bodies and through the created world, we must never suppose that we thereby receive a complete understanding of God.

So it is that, in Christian spirituality, side by side with an insistence on the possibility of knowing God through his creation, is an equal insistence that God in his supreme transcendence surpasses any human experience or thought. So it is that we say both that God acts in this way or that; he is this or that but at the same time we must say that he is not this or that; he is not to be encompassed within the limits of our human experience of him and our understanding of him. The need to recognize our limitations is not restricted to our understanding of God. Scientists who seek to understand reality have to speak in the same kind of way to insist that their expression of the nature of reality, while true, is nevertheless partial and imperfect.

So, when writing about the electron, J. Robert Oppenheimer says, 'If we ask, for instance, whether the position of the electron remains the same, we must say "no"; if we ask whether the electron's position changes with time, we must say "no"; if we ask whether the electron is at rest, we must say "no"; if we ask whether it is in motion, we must say "no" '.[3] About the need for complementary ways of speaking about reality, he says, 'These two ways of thinking, the way of time and history and the way of eternity and timelessness, are both parts of man's effort to comprehend the world in which he lives. Neither is comprehended in the other nor reducible to it. They are, as we have learned to say in physics, complementary views, each supplementing the other, neither telling the whole story'.[4]

While accepting that God surpasses our understanding, we have to speak positively. To use a word coined by the poet Gerard Manley Hopkins, we have to *inscape* into the heart of human experience and the created world to know God rather than *escape* from it. To be able to do so and to learn to do so demands that both our mind and body are under the direction of our soul. It is for this reason that we have to learn to discipline them if we are to grow and function properly in our bodies, and if what we experience in our bodies is to be consecrated to God and enable us to realize our full potential. In the process, the discipline of our bodies will reflect and take account of the way they are constructed and the way they are designed to function. Such discipline must be directed by our souls, as must be the case in the discipline of our minds. We shall be considering the nature and activity of the soul in the next chapter. For the moment, it must suffice to say that it is with our soul that we relate our experiences of mind and body to God who is our creator, who knows how we are made and whose will for us, therefore, involves the fulfilment of our bodily nature.

The New Testament speaks of the Gospel as 'the mystery'. The word is used, not in the popular sense of describing an unsolved riddle, but to describe that which has been hidden and is now revealed and which is to be known by listening, looking, and obeying, as we experience it and live in it. It makes itself known to us through our bodies as well as our minds. Reason has its part in correlating and checking the images which we receive. It can also prepare us to be aware of them but cannot create them. Our powers of reason and thought use the images and impressions which come to us through our bodies and the world in which we live. The Christian believes that it is through such images that God speaks to us. They come from the action of the divine energies and are not just the product of our imagination.

On the importance of images the holy genius Austin Farrer has written, 'The human imagination has always been controlled by certain basic images, in which man's own nature, his relation to his fellows, and his dependence upon the divine power find expression. The individual did not make them for himself. He absorbs them from the society in which he is born, partly through the suggestion of outward acts and the significance of words, partly, it would seem, by some more hidden means of apropriation. The contents of other people's finds flow into ours at a sub-conscious level, even across gaps in time and space, a fact constantly evidenced, and as constantly disbelieved. The ancestral images of which we speak may, it would seem, be carried and communicated to the next generation by those who are unaware of their existence at the conscious level. Our ignorance of what we are does not make us cease to be, and our unawareness of the profound levels of our imagination neither abolishes them nor prevents them from acting upon our wills, nor, even, on the wills and minds of others.

Who first saw life as a springing fountain, or guilt as dirt needing to be purged away? When did favourable deity begin to be an irradiating light, or divine sanctity a jewel wrapped by a veil within a veil, and guarded by jealous hands from the profane?[5]

It is the role of the poet, the artist, the musician, the dancer, to help us to see and hear the images which the world gives us if we have eyes to see and ears to hear. The use of images, metaphor and parable is however not confined to them. It is part of our normal speech as human beings, though many people do not appreciate that it is. 'It is not only poets and prophets and public speakers who use metaphor and simile to create an atmosphere in which their ideas, carried in type-images can travel still unexpressed from mind to mind. We all use metaphor as a vehicle to carry to our companion an idea which if baldly expressed would at once be killed. "He had lost his temper" states a fact, but "He was in a towering rage" presents an image which conveys an idea far more disturbing. It shares some of the undertones of "Childe Roland to the Dark Tower came": its fear and its impressiveness prepare us for disaster, whereas the alternative colloquialism (also a metaphor) "he blew his top" may describe the same scene but only introduces anti-climax. The image of the tower is archetypal – Babel 'that hideous strength', Masada, the Tower of London – and carries with it that indefinable terror which Browning exploits in Childe Roland, and Tolkien in Mordor: it is all the greater for being unexpressed.'[6]

'An idea, which is baldly expressed, would at once be killed?' For an image to convey its meaning, it has first to be experienced and received. Analysis and explanation may later help to discover other meanings, but the essential primal meaning must be received. The beauty of a rose, for example, can only be received by contemplating it and allowing it to speak to us. It cannot and will not be received simply by dissecting it to discover its structure and the way it grows. In the case of a living organism such as the human body, a knowledge of its almost inconceivable complexity may enable our experience of it to speak to us in a new way, but, having read about its inner structure, our new knowledge will not deepen our experience unless we stand back and contemplate the body for its own sake.

It is for this reason that the attempt to appreciate a poem

simply by reading an analysis of it and an examination of the poet's sources and inspiration, will not suffice. What matters above all is that we listen to the poetry itself, which by its very nature is designed to allow us to experience the impact of the images which are used. Let me give you an example. T.S. Eliot in the third movement of the first of *Four Quartets*, 'Burnt Norton,' is concerned to communicate the way in which men and women are enslaved by time. Earlier in the poem he has spoken of the attempts, always in vain, to discover the meaning of life only in the past or the future. Now, while still communicating our sense of being time-ridden, he describes how to live only in the present means living in a twilight world, without experiencing the light which illuminates or the darkness which purifies by preventing us from giving ultimate meaning to our immediate sensations. In words which are reminiscent of the procession of the damned over London Bridge in 'The Waste Land' he describes our condition.

> Here is a place of disaffection
> Time before and time after
> In a dim light: neither daylight
> Investing form with lucid stillness
> Turning shadow into transient beauty
> With slow rotation suggesting permanence
> Nor darkness to purify the soul
> Emptying the sensual with deprivation
> Cleansing affection from the temporal.
> Neither plenitude nor vacancy. Only a flicker
> Over the strained time-ridden faces
> Distracted from distraction by distraction
> Filled with fancies and empty of meaning
> Tumid apathy with no concentration

> Men and bits of paper, whirled by the cold wind
> That blows before and after time,
> Wind in and out of unwholesome lungs
> Time before and time after.

Try to rewrite that in theological or psychological terms and, though you may give more content in one way, much of the reality it conveys will be lost if, as you do it, the image is not retained. Theological or psychological terms cannot by themselves convey the reality or enable us to experience it. I shall give another example from *Four Quartets* when I come to consider the consecration of the spirit – one which speaks to us about atonement.

But let me now take a more physical example from sculpture. I remember when I was Bishop of Truro, visiting Barbara Hepworth at her home in St Ives. Some of her abstract sculptures were set in the garden into which you passed from the room in which she lived. They were there so that you could touch and feel them, for they conveyed reality as they were embraced both by eye and hand. To describe what they conveyed was impossible by word alone.

The images used by the artist, sculptor and poet, which are for the most part images we experience in our daily life but intensified to a point of revelation, enable us to take part in the exchange of life – the wondrous commerce between the life of God and the life of man. This commerce was perfectly enacted in the incarnation – the flesh-taking of God – the significance of which is proclaimed in the transfiguration where not only the body of Christ, but his clothes become translucent to the divine glory. The images all speak of the richness and complexity of human life, but they can also apeak to us of the richness and inexhaustible mystery of the divine reality from whom they have their origin.

That they may be so seen, God has given us the biblical images in his redemptive acts, which act as a kind of kaleidoscope, bringing the individual image into the glory of the divine pattern. These are the images of light and darkness, of birth and death, of sacrifice, of redemptive suffering, of covenant – the particular promise through which the universal glory is embodied. It is by these images transformed in Christ that we must be apprehended if our experience of all images is to be related to God. Such natural images as the sun, the star, the mountain are given new meaning and significance by the biblical images.

What does this say to us as we live in Christ? It says that we must see the exercise of our bodies as an integral part of our Christian life. We must see them as the sphere in which we encounter the divine energies and can co-operate with the diving creativity. What matters is that we allow the images to grasp us by our contemplation of them. We must do more than simply try to analyse them rationally.

The masters of the spiritual life speak of that moment in our life of prayer, the moment technically called the ligature, a rather unattractive description. It is when those who are called to a life of contemplative prayer become aware of the fact that they cannot think and pray at the same time. We all know that we can and must think about God and reflect upon our experience of his revelation, but there comes the moment when we know we must turn from thinking about God, our reflection upon his acts, to give our whole attention to God directly for his own sake and that we cannot do anything else at the same time. In my experience I judge that this is not a moment confined to a few chosen souls who are called to contemplation; I believe it is a very common experience of all Christians, of whom the majority are called to a simple form of contemplation, the prayer of simple attention. My experience is that many Christians know this moment. We meditate, we think about God, we think about the Scriptures, we think about the meaning of our worship and then comes the moment when we leave our thoughts and direct our being to God himself in one single, adoring act. That is the moment when our whole being, body and mind is directed by our soul towards God and we are open to him.

To allow God to speak to us we must be upright, steady, alert or perhaps kneeling, prostrate, abandoned, in loving dependence and in the wisdom of humility before God. This applies not only to our praying but also when we are listening to music, when we are listening to poetry, when we are looking at a picture, if they are to reveal the reality of which they are expressions. At such moments the whole of our being must be disciplined to that single act. That is why we must not be casual, soft, or indulgent in our attitude. As far as prayer is concerned, we must not approach God in a spirit of trying to decide whether we like his way or not.

When seeking to know God or to penetrate to the heart of created things, we shall not succeed unless we are single-minded in our approach. Perhaps we may, with Jacob and the Psalmists and Our Lord himself, wrestle in agony, piercing the darkness with our desire. To be able to receive, whether from God or the images in creation, we must be, as I say, alert not casual, body disciplined by the soul and with the mind directing itself towards God to discern how he acts with his creative energies and bestows them upon the world in which we live and speaks to us through these rich images. Not only in prayer we must be so disciplined but in our worship too. The very presence of our bodies is a necessary part of our worship. I will go so far as to say that for the Christian there is no such thing as just being there in spirit. In one sense, of course, we can, but it can never be a substitute for our presence as a living member of the body of Christ. Just as the biblical images can speak to us as we are apprehended by them through their concrete expression, just as we can understand God's loving energies through our bodies, listening to Monteverdi, to Mozart, looking at Botticelli, so I believe it is through the Sacrament, through the genuflection and the sign of the cross, through the beads slipping through the fingers, through the incense and the holy water that we are given images which we receive into our souls.

As we receive the Lord in Holy Communion, we are aware that it is the Lord giving us himself. We do not ask how, we do not ask why at that moment, we merely receive him, receive him in our being through that image of eating and drinking the Lord; through the genuflection it is as we kneel, perhaps our bones creaking in the process, that we suddenly realize that in adoration we are given a new vision of the transcendence of God. As we make the sign of the cross in thanksgiving and response to his life we feel the power of the Cross coming into our very being. As we sign ourselves with the holy water we can receive an image of the cleansing which comes in forgiveness and absolution. We direct our whole being to God so that, discerning his activity in the whole of human life, we may experience his love and his life. We learn to see that the images we encounter in human life can speak to us of Christ himself, the Lord of creation.

As we try so to live, we experience temptation and it is that of which I now speak to prepare us for the next chapter, in which we shall consider atonement.

For as we so seek to live we are faced, like our Lord, by temptation. Oscar Wilde made no bones about it. 'I can resist everything except temptation'. William Beckford, more than half a century earlier, was not so bold. He merely said, 'I am not over-fond of resisting temptation'. Robert Browning expressed a very different attitude when he wrote *The Ring and the Book:* 'Why comes temptation but for man to meet the master and make crouch beneath his foot and so be pedestalled in triumph?'

Nevertheless, these three quotations have one thing in common. They all regard temptation as leading us to do what is pleasurable but wrong, to which in the case of Oscar Wilde and Beckford it was preferable to succumb, and which in the case of Browning it was preferable to conquer. Such, I suppose, is the popular view but it is not that of Scripture, which sees temptation as a human experience arising from the nature of man – an experience which is primarily religious rather than moral, though it embraces a moral element. In Scripture, temptation is clearly distinguished from trials and tribulations on the one hand, which can have a cleansing and purifying effect upon us, as 'gold passes through the assayer's fire', and from seduction on the other, which is always willed by an enemy with evil designs. So is Revelation we read of the woman Jezebel who seduced the servants of Christ with fornication.

Temptation is seen as the inevitable experience of man, made in the image of God, with a genuine freedom to decide whether to serve him or not. The idea of temptation in the Bible expresses the spiritual tension in which every man is destined to live and die, andwhich he must recognize and accept if he is truly to live as a human being. The choices before him are real choices, each presenting something to him between which he must decide.

Many of the choices we have to make are of no ultimate significance. They may have unfortunate or awkward consequences but will not affect our eternal destiny unless they affect our relationship to God. In Scripture, the word 'temptation' is, generally speaking, confined to those that do so, when the choice before us may be presented in a simple, even seemingly trivial way, or be a very profound choice, but which, in either case, is essentially a choice between obeying and serving God, and obeying ourselves or Satan. 'I have set before you life and death: therefore choose life', is the command which God gives through Moses to the Israelites, and thus to man and woman, and temptation provides the opportunity to choose life – to choose to obey God – and it is in that positive sense that we must face it. It is in that sense that we must understand the petition in the Lord's Prayer – the choice is so vital, the danger so great, that we pray that we may not be led to the point of disobedience but delivered from the evil one.

In the wilderness, our Lord sees each temptation which he endures as the opportunity to accept the sovereign will of the Father – not just to resist the urging of Satan. On Palm Sunday he prayed, 'Now is my soul in turmoil and what am I to say? Father, save me from this hour. No, it was for this that I came to this hour'. In Gethsemane, he said to his disciples, 'Pray that you may be spared the hour of testing' and then in his agony said, 'Father, if it be thy will, take this cup away – yet not my will but thine be done'. This is the affirmation of loving obedience to the Father. We have to learn to see temptation not in a negative sense but as the opportunity to affirm our choice to serve God.

How then do we make the right choice when temptation faces us? First, of course, by availing ourselves of the promised sources of grace. While temptation is the lot of every man as is clear from the fact that Our Lord was tempted – it was an experience he shared with us in his perfect humanity – we can only make the right choice by virtue of his conquest of sin and evil and by participating in his victory. Through our union with him by Baptism, through sharing his risen life in our Communion, through the absolution of our sins, through dependence upon him by prayer, we are given what we need to enable us to choose aright.

Yet, as I say, the choice is real, our freedom is real; so are the pressures from our personal lack of holiness, from the insistence of our bodies, from the climate of opinion in which we live, from our desire to be thought well of by others who do not share our Christian discipleship, by our capitulation to an intellectual understanding of life which is not Christian. All make the choices hard. So does the fundamental difference between good and evil to which I have already referred.

The fact is that evil is essentially destructive and therefore voracious. There is no lasting value in one victory; it must be followed up by another. If we are to give in to lust it makes us weaker for the next temptation, whereas to choose to love means that we become more of a loving person, more able to choose aright next time. When temptation comes, it is quite disastrous to start arguing with yourself about it. If you start arguing with yourself about it, as to whether you can do something, you have usually given in already. Your argument will merely result in finding a reason which you think justifies you in doing it. The time for reasoning about what is right or wrong is not at the moment of temptation. What, in fact, you do is quite simple. You turn to the Lord, who is with us all the time everywhere, and you say 'Lord, is this something you want me to do?' You may not complete the question. You will realize then that you cannot think of doing this thing and think of Our Lord at the same time.

The will to choose depends largely upon our imagination or perhaps it would be better to say, our vision – the vision of the good, the vision of our own potential, the vision of eternal life. Will-power is essentially vision-power. We shall not choose aright, nor shall we respond aright to grace, unless we have the vision to see how glorious and splendid is the holiness to which we are called, but also to see the real misery of evil, its destructive nature; to see the glory of love which is eternal rather than the transitoriness of lust, to see the splendour of faithfulness and integrity rather than the immediate ease which infidelity or the breaking of promises provides. Above all we must learn to see the glory and splendour of a life shared with God rather than the misery of being left utterly alone, just with ourselves, which is the end result of successive choices to serve ourselves, and which is hell.

There are two ways of looking at temptation. The one sees it as a regrettable case of conscience to prevent us doing what seems natural and pleasurable. The other sees it as the opportunity to make a choice for God, based on our real potential of living in communion with him and becoming steadily the kind of people who reflect back to him his glory and goodness. 'My son, if you would serve God, prepare yourself for temptation'. So we read in Ecclesiastes. We must not seek it – to put ourselves to the test – or to put ourselves in the way of it. That Our Lord makes clear. But when it comes, temptation provides the opportunity to enable us to love him with 'all our heart, our mind and strength'.

THE BODY

O MY GOD, I offer to thee my body,
    which thou indeed didst fashion.

Lift it up, as my heart, to thyself:
the good desires of my mind let it translate into deed,
    the bad refuse to obey.

Let my lips be opened
> and as often kept shut, for thine honour.

Let my hands work for thee,
> my feet go about thy business.

Let my knees bend in prayer,
> and my head bow.

Let me laugh with them that laugh
> and weep with them that weep,
>> in thy Spirit of love.

Let mine eyes open to see and praise thee everywhere
>> in thy visible creation;
>> in the sons and daughters thou lovest;
> and close, to worship the King
>> immortal, invisible, only wise.

Grant me lordship, full and whole, over my body
> that I may offer it, day by day, to thee
>> in a loyal service,
>> as a sacrifice, pure and undefiled;
till it become a true temple of thy Spirit,
> ringing with the music of heaven,
> reflecting the likeness of Jesus,
>> now and always.

7

The Heart of a Christian

I have called this chapter 'The Heart of a Christian'. It would more appropriately be called the 'soul' of a Christian but I used the word 'heart' because in these days 'soul' needs explanation and justification. It is a word which is regarded as out of date, being understood as referring to the notion of some ghostly entity which is now discarded. So, in the new translation of the Scriptures we find that 'soul' is translated by such words as 'heart', 'life' or 'self', or by a paraphrase. So in the New English Bible, when Joseph's brothers speak about their brother he is described not in 'anguish of soul'. They speak of his 'suffering which we saw', words which might properly be used of an animal as well as a human being. In the Psalms God does not 'restore my soul'. Instead, 'He renews my life within me'. No longer do we say, 'Like as the hart desireth the water brooks: so longeth my soul after thee, O Lord', but 'As a hind longs for running streams: so do I long for thee, O Lord'. In the New Testament the searching question of our Lord, 'What shall it profit a man if he shall gain the whole world and lose his own soul?' is translated 'What does a man gain by winning the whole world at the cost of his true self?' In the agony in the garden of Gethsemane we no longer hear Our Lord saying 'My soul is exceeding sorrowful unto death', but, 'my heart is ready to break with grief'. When the translators have to face Hebrews 4.12 which speaks of the word of God being quick and powerful and sharper than any two-edged sword, piercing even to the dividing asunder of soul and spirit, they translate 'soul and spirit' by 'life and spirit', a distinction which is hard to understand and which misses the point that the word 'soul' refers not to a man's life or spirit but to his being made in the image of God, and to his capacity for entering into a relationship with God. It is in this sense that the masters of the spiritual life speak of the ascent of the soul. Man in his soul ascends to God as he allows what is of God to be embodied, to take shape within him and thereby to grow into the eternal reality. For Christians this growth into Christ is inseparable from sacramental union with him.

If we abolish the word 'soul' we soon find ourselves in a soulless Christianity, which in practice becomes little more than the use of the world's ways to try to solve the world's problems in time, albeit with the use of religious language. The individual becomes subjected to the institution, for, on such a basis, it is the institution which must somehow survive. The unique responsibility of the individual is eroded and the efforts of the individual must be subservient to the needs of the institution.

If, however, the individual is to take his place as a living part of the body of Christ, and so to grow into the likeness of Christ, then the fact of sin has to be faced. We must know the meaning of atonement, and to know that we must understand ourselves as we are. It is a mark of our time to look back to the past and to try to discover in our history explanations and excuses for our present condition. Although the atonement took place in a moment of time on the cross of Calvary, it is also ever present, which is merciful, for as T.S. Eliot says at the beginning of 'Burnt Norton':

> Time present and time past
> Are both perhaps present in time future
> And time future contained in time past.

> If all time is eternally present
> All time is unredeemable.
> What might have been is an abstraction
> Remaining a perpetual possibility
> Only in a world of speculation.
> What might have been and what has been
> Point to one end, which is always present.

If we look back we are disappointed,

> Footfalls echo in the memory
> Down the passage which we did not take
> Towards the door we never opened
> Into the rose-garden. My words echo
> Thus, in your mind.
>   But to what purpose
> Disturbing the dust on a bowl of rose-leaves
> I do not know.
>   Other echoes
> Inhabit the garden. Shall we follow?
> Quick, said the bird, find them, find them,
> Round the corner. Through the first gate,
> Into our first world, shall we follow
> The deception of the thrush?"

It is here and now that we need atonement. So in the second of *Four Quartets*, 'East Coker', we read:

> The wounded surgeon plies the steel
> That questions the distempered part;
> Beneath the bleeding hands we feel
> The sharp compassion of the healer's art
> Resolving the enigma of the fever chart.

Our only health is the disease
If we obey the dying nurse
Whose constant care is not to please
But to remind of our, and Adam's curse,
And that, to be restored, our sickness must grow
    worse.

The whole earth is our hospital
Endowed by the ruined millionaire,
Wherein, if we do well, we shall
Die of the absolute paternal care
That will not leave us, but prevents us everywhere.

The chill ascends from feet to knees,
The fever sings in mental wires.
If to be warmed, then I must freeze
And quake in frigid purgatorial fires
Of which the flame is roses, and the smoke is briars.

The dripping blood our only drink,
The bloody flesh our only food:
In spite of which we like to think
That we are sound, substantial flesh and blood –
Again, in spite of that, we call this Friday good.

On this passage Fr John Booty writes, 'Eliot here presents the gospel by way of an analogy devised to avoid over-used and unnecessary biblical and theological terms. Simply stated, humanity is chronically ill. The disease is sin. Sin, however defined, and Eliot defines it in various ways, is principally that self-centredness that prevents our ability to hear the gospel. (Because this sin is also the means by which we are cured, it must grow worse before it can be recognised for what it is and be excised). The cure is effected by the Lord, the wounded surgeon, who is full of compassion, who operates through the dying nurse, the Church. Eliot is careful to point out that the Church is not here to please us, but to remind us of ours in'.[1] The passage reminds us of words in the *Choruses from 'The Rock'*:

> Why should men love the Church? Why should they
>   love her laws?
> She tells them of Life and Death, and all they would
>   forget.
> She is tender where they would be hard, and hard
>   where they would be soft.
> She tells them of Evil and Sin, and other unpleasant
>   facts

But such telling is needful if atonement is to be received – received because it has already been made. I do not in any way detract from the uniqueness of the 'one oblation which Christ offered of himself, a full, perfect, and sufficient sacrifice, oblation, and satisfaction, for the sins of the whole world',[2] when I say that atonement is a two-way process. The meaning of the word makes that clear. It is the restoration to a relationship of those who were estranged. In any broken human relationship there is a price to be paid, a cost to be met if it is to be restored. Such is the case even in a casual relationship. If I collide with someone accidentally, I must say I am sorry, if the proper relationship between two persons is to be restored and we are not to go on our way in a sense of alienation. If the relationship which has been estranged was a deep one, the cost will be greater and it will not be borne equally. The greater cost will be borne by the better of the two. Because he is a more loving and holier person, he will understand more truly the meaning and significance of the estrangement which has occurred and will appreciate the cost of reconciliation. Perhaps the other man will not accept the cost at all, and rejects attempts to effect reconciliation. In that event, the better man must bear the cost of rejection while continuing to love and desire reconciliation. In a human relationship neither party can know the full reasons or the real depth of what has caused the breach, to which, perhaps, past experience of one or the other, say in childhood, may have contributed, or which may have arisen because of misunderstanding or ignorance. How often do we say, 'I am sorry; if I had known that, I would have understood how you felt'.

In our relationship to God, he knows the whole situation. He knows the ultimate significance of our sin, which alienates us from him. He knows what we are at this moment, creatures of our past, and with our expectations for the future. For him, this and every moment is the 'point of intersection of the timeless with time'. As we come to him he meets us as we are, and we can be reconciled to him with our past and our expectations for the future, though the past can, if need exist, be exorcised and our expectations transformed.

For he bears the cost. God was in Christ reconciling the world to himself. he bears the cost not only of our personal reconciliation and the forgiveness of our own sins; but that is too individualistic a way of looking at our redemption. It is the intolerable burden of the sins of the whole world, of which our sins are part, which Christ bears on Calvary. The cost of forgiving all sin is borne, and so the reconciliation is effected for the whole world for all time in Christ. 'It is love, the wounded surgeon, who endured the fire on our behalf and provides the fire that energizes us with the divine Spirit to begin again, to live anew and then to join the dance at the still point, participant in eternal life'.

It is by the Church that we are restored to health, for living in Christ, as members of his body, we know that we must die to live, both for our health and for the health of all mankind. If we are to die to live, we must live with the wounded surgeon by our side, who brings diagnosis and healing, judgment and grace. So prays a monk of the Eastern Church:

> Jesus, you are present when I sin
> And you remain in me, silent
> Your very presence condemns what I do.
> Yet at the same time, you know and understand my sin
> More profoundly than I understand myself.
> For you are more in me than I am in myself
> You do not judge me from a distance.
> You identify yourself with the sinner before you
> And yet, at this moment, you contradict what I am.
> But your presence envelopes me in boundless mercy
> . . .
> You have no need of formal sentence.
> Your presence alone, Lord
> Is the judgement which condemns me.
> But your presence is also grace.
> There could be no word of grace
> If there was no word of judgment.[3]

How then comes the judgment? Through the Word made flesh who is the light of the world. He came not to condemn the world but to save it. True, but judgment and condemnation are not the same thing. Both condemnation and forgiveness can only come after judgment. But the judgment of the Word is the revelation of the judgment of God, just as it is the work of the Spirit of truth to speak not of his own authority but of what the Word has spoken, so that the judgment is made, so that atonement may follow.

'So Jesus cried aloud: "When a man believes in me, he believes in him who sent me rather than in me; seeing me, he sees him who sent me. I have come into the world as light, so that no one who has faith in me should remain in darkness. But if anyone hears my words and pays no regard to them, I am not his judge; I have not come to judge the world, but to save the world. There is a judge for the man who rejects me and does not accept my words; the word that I spoke will be his judge on the last day. I do not speak on my own authority, but the Father who sent me has himself commanded me what to say and how to speak. I know that his commands are eternal life. What the Father has said to me, therefore – that is what I speak" '. (John 12.44–50)

'I know that his commands are eternal life'. The Lord came not to destroy the law but to fulfil it. We cannot hear what the Lord says to us about the inner meaning of the law unless we know the law. It is for this reason that a Christian cannot regard himself above the law. But as we hear the law in Christ, we hear both the judgment and the fulfilment. By the law we stand judged, even on its literal meaning but in Christ we hear its deeper meaning and see it as the expression of love, so that obedience to the law can never, by itself, enable us to live in one with reality. In Christ, we hear its deepest meaning. We stand under its judgment but also under the judgment of Christ. But we are, in Christ, given the freedom to obey, for he lived and died in the law but in love for the Father.

Let us return to the Church in which we live. T.S. Eliot describes her as the 'dying nurse', which may seem surprising. Surely, some will say, the Church should live in the joy of the resurrection with the experience of eternal life. Yes indeed, but there was no resurrection without the cross. The risen life demands both a daily dying to sin and the ability to suffer creatively. She is above all the sacrificial body, the body that has been slain to rise again, dying the death to rise in glory, the body set in the world through which the 'wounded surgeon' continues his work. By being the sacrificial body, the Church can be the community in which redemption takes place, in which hatred is replaced by love, in which forgiveness is offered and received, in which all life is consecrated in truth to God.

At the heart of its life is the eucharistic action, through which we are enabled to do two things. They are beautifully expressed by Irenaeus, who was Bishop of Lyons and lived from about AD 130–200. In his book, *Against Heresies*, he wrote:

> 'And because we are his members and are nourished by what is created he who makes his sun rise on and rains on whom ever he chooses providing us with a created thing when he declares the cup taken from created things which causes our blood to flow, to be his Blood and the bread taken from created things, from which he gives growth to our bodies, he affirms to be his Body. Therefore when the wine mixed with water and the baked bread receive the Word of God and the Eucharist becomes the Body of Christ, and the substance of our flesh grows and is sustained by these elements, how can they deny that our flesh is capable of receiving the gift of God, which is eternal life, since it is nourished by the Body and Blood of Christ and is a member of it?'[4]

We have to offer the world to God that through the action of the Word and its reception by us, it may become part of the new creation. We ourselves have to live as members of the sacrificial body in which the new creation is lived.

You will recall how St Paul bids us recollect the meaning of our Baptism. 'What are we to say, then? Shall we persist in sin, so that there may be all the more grace? No, no! We died to sin: how can we live in it any longer? Have you forgotten that when we were baptized into union with Christ Jesus we were baptized into his death? By baptism we were buried with him, and lay dead, in order that, as Christ was raised from the dead in the splendour of the Father, so also we might set our feet upon the new path of life. For if we have become incorporate with him in a death like his, we shall also be one with him in a resurrection like his. We know that the man we once were has been crucified with Christ, for the destruction of the sinful self, so that we may no longer be the slaves of sin, since a dead man is no longer answerable for his sin. But if we thus died with Christ, we believe that we shall also come to life with him. We know that Christ, once raised from the dead, is never to die again: he is no longer under the dominion of death. For in dying as he died, he died to sin, once for all, and in living as he lives, he lives to God. In the same way you must regard yourselves as dead to sin and alive to God, in union with Christ Jesus'. (Romans 6.1-11)

It is by our participation in the Eucharist that we live out the meaning of our Baptism. We participate because we are reconciled to God, through the sacrifice in which the cost of our reconciliation is borne. Yet to be sacrificed ourselves with Christ is for us the acceptance that the cost has been borne. So St Peter can say, 'For it is a fine thing if a man endure the pain of undeserved suffering because God is in his thoughts. What credit is there in fortitude when you have done wrong and are beaten for it? But when you have behaved well and suffer for it, your fortitude is a fine thing in the sight of God.

To that you were called, because Christ suffered on your behalf, and thereby left you an example; it is for you to follow in his steps. He committed no sin, he was convicted of no falsehood; when he was abused he did not retort with abuse, when he suffered he uttered no threats, but committed his cause to the One who judges justly. In his own person he carried our sins to the gibbet, so that we might cease to live for sin and begin to live for righteousness. By his wounds you have been healed. You were straying like sheep, but now you have turned towards the Shepherd and the Guardian of your souls'. (1 Peter 2.19–25)

The devotion of our soul involves a sharing in that way of exchange, that way of exchange by which there comes beauty from ashes, the oil of joy for mourning and the garment of praise for the spirit of heaviness, for these things come when, with singlemindedness of purpose, we relate all things to God and bring them to him for consecration in Christ.

CONSECRATION

O GOD, give me desire,
>> overmastering and perpetual,
> to consecrate myself to thee,
>> my life to thy Kingdom,
>> my love to all whom thou lovest.

Grant me, O my Father,
> not desire only
>> but obedience to match,
> and power to oblation,
>> through the very Spirit of Jesus.

This day give me grace
> to lift up my soul,
> to pray without ceasing,
> to wait upon thy good pleasure;
to hear thy voice, speak thy word, do thy will,
> seek thy forgiveness.

And if I have little or nought else to offer,
> accept my faith,
and keep it unswerving, unafraid, burning
> to welcome thy demands,
>> and their cost.

8

In the Image of God

'Human kind cannot bear very much reality'. So says T.S. Eliot in the first of the *Four Quartets*. And he is right, and yet man seeks reality to give meaning to his life. And, as we have seen, man is made for an eternal relationship with reality, God who is love. But man clutches at what he supposes to be reality in a form which he can encompass and control. He grasps substitutes, many of which are good and not to be despised, yet which, having no ultimate substance in themselves, cannot take the strain. Both images, such as the sun or thunder and lightning, and abstract notions, such as beauty or justice, have been used as substitutes for reality. In both cases, there is a difference between those which represent some aspects of man's desires or needs and those which represent some one or some thing outside man which challenges him. The former are not religious in the proper sense of that word. Money, as the image of power, is essentially inward looking to man's desires. For humanism, with its rejection of the supernatural, man is paramount. The notions of law, truth, justice and religion can and do represent acceptance of standards and demands outside man. What Eliot says of the words which we use to describe these reflections of reality, describe our experience with the things themselves.

> Words strain,
> Crack and sometimes break, under the burden,
> Under the tension, slip, slide, perish,

> Decay with imprecision, will not stay in place,
> Will not stay still.

Law is the sinew of tradition – essential, indispensable – without which mankind slips into anarchy. Yet, if made the only basis of our life, it becomes a harsh, inhuman, rigid frame denying us our liberty. The Lord recalls us to the source of law which also gives it life. The source is love, the love of God, by which we are inspired to minister the law not only with justice and mercy but in the spirit – in its very depths. So law is to be seen not as the application of impersonal principles, the expression of the dictates of a tyrant, whether individual or corporate, or as the means by which we seek to get our way, but as the means of justice. 'We have a law and by that law he ought to die'. Law by itself leads to crucifixion and will not stand as the representative of reality.

But neither will justice bear the strain. To be human is to be able to choose between different causes of action and to have the responsibility of accepting the consequences of those decisions. Yet both the choices we have to make and the consequences which may follow are not the result of our acts alone. Others affect our choices, we affect theirs. We bear the consequences of the acts of others and they bear ours. Our dependence upon one another, even upon those whom we never see and of whom we may never have heard; the predictability of the physical world, upon which we rely to exercise our freedom yet which must, of necessity, be the same for all; these make human justice a blunt instrument and cause the Psalmist to ask, with men and women throughout the ages, why the ungodly flourish like a green bay tree.

What then of truth? 'What is truth' says jesting Pilate and tarries not for answer. He answers the question by his actions, which reveal the inadequacy of truth as expressed by human kind. By the truth of the Roman law, he finds no crime in Jesus. By the Jewish custom of the release of a prisoner at the Passover, which expresses the demand of truth that justice must be tempered by mercy, he releases Barabbas and thereby delivers Jesus to be crucified. For while man must seek to live by the truth, he must also accept that what he offers as truth are but approximations to it, pale and sometimes distorted reflections of it. Nor is it to be found simply in words, for words 'slip, slide, parish'. It springs out of the earth, in the order and beauty of that which God has created. The God of eternal reality stands over us all as we seek to express the truth. He is the truth and we stand judged.

Truth, justice, law, none of these three will provide in themselves the reality for which man seek. Such is the case with all man's principles and activities, as Eliot makes clear with sharp poetic precision in the second of the Quartets, 'East Coker'.

> The captains, merchant bankers, eminent men of letters,
> The generous patrons of art, the statesmen and the rulers,
> Distinquished civil servants, chairmen of many committees,
> Industrial lords and petty contractors, all go into the dark,
> And dark the Sun and Moon, and the Almanach de Gotha
> And the Stock Exchange Gazette, the Directory of Directors,
> And cold the sense, and lost the motive of action.
> And we all go with them, into the silent funeral,
> Nobody's funeral, for there is no one to bury.

And what is true of these is true of religion. For commercial transactions to take place in the temple did not give them an unassailable propriety, did not give them an unquestionable validity. So the Lord cleansed the temple but, more, the temple itself had to be destroyed and rebuilt, not with stones but in the body of the Lord. The temple, religion itself, can arrogate to itself the claim to reality apart from God and then dark things can be done in its name.

Religion, like truth, justice and law, has to give its power back to God if it is not to be corrupted and used for purposes which are 'alien' to his mind. The pursuit of each as an end in itself, however necessary each be to human life, leads to darkness, darkness where there is no ultimate ground for hope, no security, nothing of worth in which to put one's final trust.

Where then is reality to be found? In God alone, the source of all reality, who alone gives ultimate meaning to all things and all people. God alone, who needs no reason to exist but gives reason to everything else. If our human nature is to be redeemed; if the principalities, the rulers of the darkness of this world which derive their power from our attempts to seek reality in that which is not, are to be defeated; if man is to be delivered from the darkness and, more important, to be enabled to live freely and lovingly in union with God who is reality, someone must freely and lovingly endure the darkness, to cleave to God in it and through it, to defeat it and to share his victory with others.

So Jesus, God and man, who had gone about teaching, healing and doing all manner of good among the people, comes to the moment when he sets his face towards Jerusalem. In his public ministry the Holy Spirit, for the first time, dwelt in one on earth who was wholly obedient to his promptings. Our Lord brought the creative and redeeming power of God to bear upon those whom he met. As he did so, his actions reflected our human situation. At times he healed, almost it seems without condition, as if recognizing that the person's state was not his fault but sprang from that dependence on one another of which I spoke earlier, and on the predictability of the created world, which does not distinguish between the good and the bad. At other times he discerned that there was an underlying spiritual cause and called for repentance and obedience.

His mission was not, however, to be limited to the few. Nor did he come simply to be an example from which those of later generations might benefit. He came to give new life – to recreate man and the universe.

So there came that moment when he said, 'Behold, we go up to Jerusalem'. It was the moment from which he went forward to defeat the powers of sin and evil. Although he was to put himself into the hands of his enemies, it was also to be 'his hour'. He was to accept the worst that they could bring upon him but he was to remain unconquered and to demonstrate that for man to put himself wholly in the hands of God leads not to destruction but to transformation. He, the Word, by whom all things were made, was to effect the new creation.

In the Scriptures, darkness is the great symbol of being separated from God. So, before God calls into being that which was to reflect his glory and receive life from him, 'darkness was upon the face of the deep'. The Spirit of God moved upon the waters and God said, 'Let there be light, and there was light'. Men 'loved the darkness rather than the light'. So the earth was corrupt in God's sight and the earth was filled with violence. When Abraham is called by God to go forth from his own country, to become the father of the nation through whom all mankind will be blessed and receive the covenant of God's promise, he prepares an offering. Then 'a horror of great darknes falls upon him', for man cannot make the offering he should. In the darkness there passes through the offering the smoking pot and the flaming torch, signs of the divine presence which cleaves the darkness, and through which the offering can and will be made.

So, before the deliverance of the people of Israel from their captivity in Egypt, there was thick darkness over the land.

Now, in Jerusalem, as the true Exodus was to be effected, the darkness descended. 'Now it was about the sixth hour and there was darkness over the whole world until the ninth hour'. But it was more than a physical darkness, for the incarnate God was numbered with those whom the law regards as transgressors and religion regards as blasphemous. Deserted by his disciples, mocked, scourged and spat upon, he was then crucified. Physical suffering, spiritual anguish of betrayal and abondonment by his own, even the anguish of seeing man pursuing to the end his rejection of God, are as nothing compared with what he endured when the final darkness fell and he descended into the abyss. There he experienced the ultimate state of alienation from the source of his being as man. 'The darkness into which Jesus descended was a darkness of the spirit'. In human measures of time the evangelist tells us it lasted three hours and thus the Church commemorates it. But in suffering, it was timeless, as eternity of anguish. 'My God, my God why hast thou forsaken me?' We are confronted here with the ineffable mystery of divine suffering at the heart of revelation.

'Death's powers do their worst'. He endured the double agony. We would be guilty of the bitter sin of ingratitude if we were to attempt to minimize the physical suffering of Our Lord but I believe we do well not to contemplate it unduly, for it is not that which is at the heart of the cross which is to be found in the sharing of our separation at the heart of being, through the moment of death. At that moment, even in the separation, the love of God for man, and the love of man for God prevailed. 'The light shines in the darkness and the darkness does not overcome it'.

Now the Lord himself spoke of the way in which a seed of corn must die if it is to be changed into the plant of wheat, to bear fruit and to be brought to fulfilment. Theologians and poets have turned to the transformation of the chrysalis into a butterfly, or the larva to a dragonfly, as signs of a death which rises in glory. Marvellous though such changes are, such that we are tempted to use the word miraculous, miracles they are not. They are but the expression in our natural world of the energies of God who directs and sustains its life.

When the creator himself, the Word made flesh, takes our human life, body, mind and spirit through death, giving it back in perfect trust to the Father from whom it comes, to whom it belongs, then indeed a miracle is wrought. 'Christ was raised up from the dead by the glory of the Father' (Romans 6.4 AV), and in Christ our human nature is glorified in union with the life of God. All that was necessary for Christ to be truly man becomes transparent to the divine will and glory.

When St Paul says, 'As in Adam all die, even so in Christ shall all be made alive', (1 Cor. 15.22 AV), he is speaking not merely of the sharing of Christ in our humanity. He is speaking of Christ as inaugurating the new creation, the beginning of a new race and of its fulfilment. He is the first fruits of life liberated and consummated in God.

And in that fulfilment all that we have experienced and known of God in human life will be brought to perfection. The bodily resurrection of Our Lord prevents us from despising the craftsman's skill, the seeing eye, the delight in beauty, the caring hand, or despairing lest what they reveal and express of the glory of God in this life should be lost in life beyond the grave. Purged of all selfishness and imperfection, what we enjoy through them will be fulfilled as the means of sharing in the divine glory.

Even now, the power of the risen Lord is given and experienced through our bodies. The water flows over us in Baptism, we are cleansed and united to him. We eat and drink the sacrament of his Body and his Blood and, mysteriously, the whole of our being is renewed in union with him. Through such acts of grace, full realization of our destiny, our transformation to be living sacraments of the divine glory can begin.

This life of space and time is to be redeemed, not by a release into a phantasmal world, nor by the grim prospect of endlessness. It will be redeemed by its fulfilment in Christ in which the whole of our being, shaped in space and time, will, beyond both, realize its true potential, reflecting back to God in love his glory.

Life for Jesus is life lived for the Father, which he calls us to share.

I return to T.S. Eliot:

> We shall not cease from exploration
> And the end of all our exploring
> Will be to arrive where we started
> And know the place for the first time

Jesus said, 'I came out from the Father and am come into the world: again, I leave the world, and go to the Father'. 'Now, O Father, glorify thou me with thine own self with the glory I had with thee before the world began'.

We come from God, ultimate reality, the source of all being and the sustainer of all life. We are made for God, and in

Christ we can go to God. To arrive in Christ, united to him in his glorious body, is to arrive where we started, for he is the Word by whom all things were made. It is to know the place for the first time, for in him we see and share the glory.

> When the tongues of flame are unfolded
> Into the crowned knot of fire
> And the fire and rose are one.

JUBILA DEO

LET ME SING unto the Lord,
   sing praises joyfully unto the Most High:
sing to the Lord of all the earth,
sing to the Lord of the whole heavens,
   sing a new song unto the Lord my God.

Never will I cease to sing praises
        unto my God:
sing with words and without words,
sing in the daytime and in the dark,
sing with my understanding and with my heart,
   rehearse with my whole being my song,
All my fresh springs shall be in thee, O Lord.

—Rehearse it with the choirs of heaven
        and with their joy.
From the eternal let it ring
   through the transiencies of every day.
To the eternal let it leap,
   from thee and to thee, O my God!

THOU, O Father almighty, thou art my song;
THOU, O Son my Saviour, thou its theme;

THOU, O Spirit of Love, its stream and melody.
O Holy, Blessed, and Glorious Trinity,
   lift my praises to the heavenly choirs
      even now; and always.

Notes

Chapter 2
1. G. Leonard, *God Alive*, DLT, 1981, p.61
2. ibid, p.63
3. J. Lowe, *The Lord's Prayer*, Oxford, 1962, p.12

Chapter 3
1. Athanasius, *The Incarntion of the Word of God*, Bles, E.T., 1944, p.41
2. A.C. McGill, *The Celebration of Flesh*, Peter Smith, 1964, p.32
3. J.A.T. Robinson, *The Body*, SCM, 1952, p.15
4. E.L. Mascall, *The Centrality of Mary*, Walsingham Assumptiontide Lecture, 1979, p.2
5. J.A.T. Robinson, op. cit., p.51
6. ibid.
7. A. Schweitzer, *The Mysticism of Paul the Apostle*, 1930, p.285
8. ibid.

Chapter 4
1. Paul Brand and Philip Yancey, *Fearfully and Wonderfully Made*, Hodder Stoughton, 1981
   Paul Brand and Philip Yancey, *In His Image*, Hodder & Stoughton, 1984
2. C.F.D. Moule, *The Phenomenon of the New Testament*, SCM, 1967, p.26

Chapter 5
1. J.K. Mozley, *Essay on 'The Bible: Its Unity Inspiration and Authority'* in *The Christian Faith*, Ed. W.R. Matthews, SPCK, 1936, p.43
2. See, for example, Ghita Ionescu, *Politics and Human Happiness*, Longmans, 1984

3. R.E. Brown, *Biblical Exegesis and Church Doctrine*, Geoffrey Chapman, 1985, p.21
4. Cambridge Sermons, *The Language of the Church* SPCK, 1985, p.90
5. H. Blamires, *The Christian Mind*, SPCK, 1963, pp.44-45

Chapter 6
1. Jean Mouroux, *The Meaning of Man*, Sheed & Ward, ET, 1948, p.43
2. G.L. Prestige, *The Life of Charles Gore*, Heinemann, 1935, p.466
3. J. Robert Oppenheimer, *Science and the Common Understanding*, New York, 1954, p.40
4. ibid p.69
5. Austin Farrer, *A Rebirth of Images*, Dacre, 1949, p.13
6. H.A. Blair, *The Kaleidoscope of Truth*, Churchman Publishing Co., 1986, p.16

Chapter 7
1. John Booty, *Meditating on Four Quartets*, Cowley Publications USA, 1983, p.27
2. Book of Common Prayer – Prayer of Consecration
3. *The Unity Book of Prayers*, Chapman, 1969, p.33
4. Irenaeus, *Against Heresies*, V2.2, tr. R.P.C. Hanson

For Further Reading

A. *Commentaries*
Genesis, Derek Kidner, Tyndale Press, 1967
Psalms, Derek Kidner, Tyndale Press, 2 vols. 1973 and 1975
Companion to the New Testament, New English Bible, A.E. Harvey, Oxford, 1970
Acts, J. Howard Marshall, Tyndale Press, 1980
1 Corinthians, John Ruef, Penguin Books, 1971
John, F.F. Bruce, Pickering Paperbacks, 1983
1 John, F.F. Bruce, Pickering, 1970

B.
Fearfully and Wonderfully Made, Paul Braund and Philip Yancey, Hodder & Stoughton, 1982
In His Image, Paul Braund and Philip Yancey, Hodder & Stoughton, 1982
The World as Sacrament, Alexander Schemann, Darton Longman & Todd, 1966
Prayer – Vol. 1 Living with God, Simon Tugwell O.P., Veritas, Dublin, 1974
Holiness, Donald Nicholl, Darton Longman and Todd, 1981
The Way of the Heart, Henri J.M. Nouwen, D.L.T., 1981
Jesus – Who He is and How We Know Him, E.L. Mascall, D.L.T., 1985
Longing for the Heavenly Realm, P. Toon, Hodder & Stoughton, 1986
Reflections on the Psalms, C.S. Lewis, Bles, 1958